Cram101 Textbook Outlines to accompany:

Parenthood and Mental Health : A bridge between infant and adult psychiatry

Sam Tyano, 1st Edition

A Content Technologies Inc. publication (c) 2012.

Learning System

Cram101 Textbook Outlines is a learning system. The notes in this book are the highlights of your textbook, you will never have to highlight a book again.

How to use this book. Take this book to class, it is your notebook for the lecture. The notes and highlights on the left hand side of the pages follow the outline and order of the textbook. All you have to do is follow along while your instructor presents the lecture. Circle the items emphasized in class and add other important information on the right side. With Cram101 Textbook Outlines you'll spend less time writing and more time listening. Learning becomes more efficient.

Cram101.com Online

Increase your studying efficiency by using Cram101.com's practice tests and online reference material. It is the perfect complement to Cram101 Textbook Outlines. Use self-teaching matching tests or simulate in-class testing with comprehensive multiple choice tests, or simply use Cram's true and false tests for quick review. Cram101.com even allows you to enter your in-class notes for an integrated studying format combining the textbook notes with your class notes.

Visit **www.Cram101.com**, click Sign Up at the top of the screen, and enter **DK73DW16506** in the promo code box on the registration screen. Your access to www.Cram101.com is discounted by 50% because you have purchased this book. Sign up and stop highlighting textbooks forever.

 ISBN(s): 9781428859913. PUBE-6.2011311

Parenthood and Mental Health : A bridge between infant and adult psychiatry
Sam Tyano, 1st

CONTENTS

Chapter 1. Parental Orientations

Infant	An infant is the very young offspring of humans. A newborn is an infant who is within hours, days, or up to a few weeks from birth. In medical contexts, newborn or neonate refers to an infant in the first 28 days of life (from birth up to 4 weeks after birth, less than a month old).
Child development	Child development refers to the biological and psychological changes that occur in human beings between birth and the end of adolescence, as the individual progresses from dependency to increasing autonomy. Because these developmental changes may be strongly influenced by genetic factors and events during prenatal life, genetics and prenatal development are usually included as part of the study of child development. Related terms include developmental psychology, referring to development throughout the lifespan, and pediatrics, the branch of medicine relating to the care of children. Developmental change may occur as a result of genetically-controlled processes known as maturation, or as a result of environmental factors and learning, but most commonly involves an interaction between the two.
Infertility	Infertility primarily refers to the biological inability of a person to contribute to conception. Infertility may also refer to the state of a woman who is unable to carry a pregnancy to full term. There are many biological causes of infertility, some which may be bypassed with medical intervention. Women who are fertile experience a natural period of fertility before and during ovulation, and they are naturally infertile during the rest of the menstrual cycle. Fertility awareness methods are used to discern when these changes occur by tracking changes in cervical mucus or basal body temperature.
Paradigm	The word paradigm has been used in science to describe distinct concepts. It comes from Greek "παρ?δειγμα" (paradeigma), "pattern, example, sample" from the verb "παραδε? κνυμι" (paradeiknumi), "exhibit, represent, expose" and that from "παρ?" (para), "beside, by" + "δε?κνυμι" (deiknumi), "to show, to point out". The original Greek term παραδε?γματι (paradeigma) was used in Greek texts such as Plato's Timaeus (28A) as the model or the pattern that the Demiurge (god) used to create the cosmos.
Reuptake	Reuptake is the reabsorption of a neurotransmitter by a neurotransmitter transporter of a pre-synaptic neuron after it has performed its function of transmitting a neural impulse.

Reuptake is necessary for normal synaptic physiology because it allows for the recycling of neurotransmitters and regulates the level of neurotransmitter present in the synapse and controls how long a signal resulting from neurotransmitter release lasts. Because neurotransmitters are too large and hydrophilic to diffuse through the membrane, specific transport proteins are necessary for the reabsorption of neurotransmitters. Much research, both biochemical and structural, has been performed to obtain clues about the mechanism of reuptake.

Selective serotonin reuptake inhibitor

Selective serotonin reuptake inhibitors or serotonin-specific reuptake inhibitor are a class of compounds typically used as antidepressants in the treatment of depression, anxiety disorders, and some personality disorders. They are also typically effective and used in treating some cases of insomnia.

Selective serotonin reuptake inhibitors are believed to increase the extracellular level of the neurotransmitter serotonin by inhibiting its reuptake into the presynaptic cell, increasing the level of serotonin in the synaptic cleft available to bind to the postsynaptic receptor.

Serotonin

Serotonin is a monoamine neurotransmitter. Biochemically derived from tryptophan, serotonin is primarily found in the gastrointestinal (GI) tract, platelets, and in the central nervous system (CNS) of animals including humans. It is a well-known contributor to feelings of well-being; therefore it is also known as a "happiness hormone" despite not being a hormone.

Stillbirth

A stillbirth occurs when a fetus has died in the uterus. The Australian definition specifies that fetal death is termed a stillbirth after 20 weeks gestation or the baby weighs more than 400 grams (14 oz). Once the baby has died the mother still has contractions and the baby is delivered. The term is often used in distinction to live birth or miscarriage. Most stillbirths occur in full term pregnancies.

Withdrawal

Withdrawal can refer to any sort of separation, but is most commonly used to describe the group of symptoms that occurs upon the abrupt discontinuation/separation or a decrease in dosage of the intake of medications, recreational drugs, and/or alcohol. In order to experience the symptoms of withdrawal, one must have first developed a physical dependence (often referred to as chemical dependency). This happens after consuming one or more of these substances for a certain period of time, which is both dose dependent and varies based upon the drug consumed.

Domestic violence	Domestic violence can be broadly defined as a pattern of abusive behaviors by one or both partners in an intimate relationship such as marriage, dating, family, friends or cohabitation. Domestic violence has many forms including physical aggression (hitting, kicking, biting, shoving, restraining, slapping, throwing objects), or threats thereof; sexual abuse; emotional abuse; controlling or domineering; intimidation; stalking; passive/covert abuse (e.g., neglect); and economic deprivation. Alcohol consumption and mental illness can be co-morbid with abuse, and present additional challenges when present alongside patterns of abuse.
Depression	Depression is a state of low mood and aversion to activity that can affect a person's thoughts, behaviour, feelings and physical well-being. It may include feelings of sadness, anxiety, emptiness, hopelessness, worthlessness, guilt, irritability, or restlessness. Depressed people may lose interest in activities that once were pleasurable, experience difficulty concentrating, remembering details, or making decisions, and may contemplate or attempt suicide.
Intervention	An intervention is an orchestrated attempt by one, or often many, people (usually family and friends) to get someone to seek professional help with an addiction or some kind of traumatic event or crisis, or other serious problem. The term intervention is most often used when the traumatic event involves addiction to drugs or other items. Intervention can also refer to the act of using a technique within a therapy session.
Child care	Child care means caring for and supervising children usually from 0-8 years of age. In the United States child care is increasingly referred to as early childhood education due to the understanding of the impact of early experiences of the developing child. Child care is a broad topic covering a wide spectrum of contexts, activities, social and cultural conventions, and institutions.
Monoamine oxidase inhibitor	Monoamine oxidase inhibitors (MAOIs) are a class of antidepressant drugs prescribed for the treatment of depression. They are particularly effective in treating atypical depression. Because of potentially lethal dietary and drug interactions, monoamine oxidase inhibitors have historically been reserved as a last line of treatment, used only when other classes of antidepressant drugs (for example selective serotonin reuptake inhibitors and tricyclic antidepressants) have failed.

Mental disorder	A mental disorder is a psychological or behavioral pattern generally associated with subjective distress or disability that occurs in an individual, and which is not a part of normal development or culture. The recognition and understanding of mental health conditions has changed over time and across cultures, and there are still variations in the definition, assessment, and classification of mental disorders, although standard guideline criteria are widely accepted. A few mental disorders are diagnosed based on the harm to others, regardless of the subject's perception of distress.
Sleep disorder	A sleep disorder is a medical disorder of the sleep patterns of a person or animal. Some sleep disorders are serious enough to interfere with normal physical, mental and emotional functioning. A test commonly ordered for some sleep disorders is the polysomnography.
Arousal	Arousal is a physiological and psychological state of being awake or reactive to stimuli. It involves the activation of the reticular activating system in the brain stem, the autonomic nervous system and the endocrine system, leading to increased heart rate and blood pressure and a condition of sensory alertness, mobility and readiness to respond. There are many different neural systems involved in what is collectively known as the arousal system.
Beck Depression Inventory	The Beck Depression Inventory created by Dr. Aaron T. Beck, is a 21-question multiple-choice self-report inventory, one of the most widely used instruments for measuring the severity of depression. Its development marked a shift among health care professionals, who had until then viewed depression from a psychodynamic perspective, instead of it being rooted in the patient's own thoughts. In its current version the questionnaire is designed for individuals aged 13 and over, and is composed of items relating to symptoms of depression such as hopelessness and irritability, cognitions such as guilt or feelings of being punished, as well as physical symptoms such as fatigue, weight loss, and lack of interest in sex.

Psychodynamics	Psychodynamics is the theory and systematic study of the psychological forces that underlie human behavior, especially the dynamic relations between conscious motivation and unconscious motivation. The psychologist Sigmund Freud (1856-1939) developed "psychodynamics" to describe the processes of the mind as flows of psychological energy (Libido) in an organically complex brain. In medical praxis, psychodynamic psychotherapy is a less intensive, 3-5 weekly sessions, than the classical Freudian psychoanalysis treatment of only one weekly session.
Anxiety	Anxiety is a psychological and physiological state characterized by somatic, emotional, cognitive, and behavioral components. The root meaning of the word anxiety is 'to vex or trouble'; in either the absence or presence of psychological stress, anxiety can create feelings of fear, worry, uneasiness and dread. Anxiety is considered to be a normal reaction to stress.
Anxiety disorder	Anxiety disorders are blanket terms covering several different forms of abnormal and pathological fear and anxiety which only came under the aegis of psychiatry at the very end of the 19th century. Gelder, Mayou ' Geddes (2005) explains that anxiety disorders are classified in two groups: continuous symptoms and episodic symptoms. Current psychiatric diagnostic criteria recognize a wide variety of anxiety disorders.
Competence	In American law, competence concerns the mental capacity of an individual to participate in legal proceedings. Defendants that do not possess sufficient "competence" are usually excluded from criminal prosecution, while witnesses found not to possess requisite competence cannot testify. The English equivalent is fitness to plead.
Fetal alcohol syndrome	Fetal/Foetal alcohol syndrome is a pattern of mental and physical defects that can develop in a fetus when a woman drinks alcohol during pregnancy. The timing and frequency of alcohol consumption during pregnancy are major factors in the risk of a child developing fetal alcohol syndrome. While the ingestion of alcohol does not always result in Fetal alcohol syndrome, there are no medically established guidelines for safe levels of alcohol consumption during pregnancy.

Generalized anxiety disorder	Generalized anxiety disorder is an anxiety disorder that is characterized by excessive, uncontrollable and often irrational worry about everyday things that is disproportionate to the actual source of worry. This excessive worry often interferes with daily functioning, as individuals suffering Generalized anxiety disorder typically anticipate disaster, and are overly concerned about everyday matters such as health issues, money, death, family problems, friend problems, relationship problems or work difficulties. They often exhibit a variety of physical symptoms, including fatigue, fidgeting, headaches, nausea, numbness in hands and feet, muscle tension, muscle aches, difficulty swallowing, bouts of difficulty breathing, difficulty concentrating, trembling, twitching, irritability, agitation, sweating, restlessness, insomnia, hot flashes, and rashes and inability to fully control the anxiety.
Alcohol Use Disorders Identification Test	The Alcohol Use Disorders Identification Test is a simple ten-question test developed by the World Health Organization to determine if a person's alcohol consumption may be harmful. The test was designed to be used internationally, and was validated in a study using patients from six countries. Questions 1-3 deal with alcohol consumption, 4-6 relate to alcohol dependence and 7-10 consider alcohol related problems.
Identification	Identification is a psychological process whereby the subject assimilates an aspect, property, or attribute of the other and is transformed, wholly or partially, after the model the other provides. It is by means of a series of identifications that the personality is constituted and specified. The roots of the concept can be found in Freud's writings.
Pain	Pain is "an unpleasant sensory and emotional experience associated with actual or potential tissue damage, or described in terms of such damage." It is the feeling common to such experiences as stubbing a toe, burning a finger, putting iodine on a cut, and bumping the "funny bone". Pain motivates us to withdraw from potentially damaging situations, protect a damaged body part while it heals, and avoid those situations in the future. Most pain resolves promptly once the painful stimulus is removed and the body has healed, but sometimes pain persists despite removal of the stimulus and apparent healing of the body; and sometimes pain arises in the absence of any detectable stimulus, damage or disease.

Nicotine

Nicotine is an alkaloid found in the nightshade family of plants (Solanaceae) that constitutes approximately 0.6-3.0% of the dry weight of tobacco, with biosynthesis taking place in the roots and accumulation occurring in the leaves. It functions as an antiherbivore chemical with particular specificity to insects; therefore nicotine was widely used as an insecticide in the past, and currently nicotine analogs such as imidacloprid continue to be widely used. Nicotine is also found in several other members of the Solanaceae family, with small amounts being present in species such as the eggplant and tomato.

Smoking

Smoking is a practice in which a substance, most commonly tobacco or cannabis, is burned and the smoke is tasted or inhaled. This is primarily practised as a route of administration for recreational drug use, as combustion releases the active substances in drugs such as nicotine and makes them available for absorption through the lungs. It can also be done as a part of rituals, to induce trances and spiritual enlightenment.

Chapter 2. Challenging pregnancies

Infant

An infant is the very young offspring of humans. A newborn is an infant who is within hours, days, or up to a few weeks from birth. In medical contexts, newborn or neonate refers to an infant in the first 28 days of life (from birth up to 4 weeks after birth, less than a month old).

Withdrawal

Withdrawal can refer to any sort of separation, but is most commonly used to describe the group of symptoms that occurs upon the abrupt discontinuation/separation or a decrease in dosage of the intake of medications, recreational drugs, and/or alcohol. In order to experience the symptoms of withdrawal, one must have first developed a physical dependence (often referred to as chemical dependency). This happens after consuming one or more of these substances for a certain period of time, which is both dose dependent and varies based upon the drug consumed.

Depression

Depression is a state of low mood and aversion to activity that can affect a person's thoughts, behaviour, feelings and physical well-being. It may include feelings of sadness, anxiety, emptiness, hopelessness, worthlessness, guilt, irritability, or restlessness. Depressed people may lose interest in activities that once were pleasurable, experience difficulty concentrating, remembering details, or making decisions, and may contemplate or attempt suicide.

Intervention

An intervention is an orchestrated attempt by one, or often many, people (usually family and friends) to get someone to seek professional help with an addiction or some kind of traumatic event or crisis, or other serious problem. The term intervention is most often used when the traumatic event involves addiction to drugs or other items. Intervention can also refer to the act of using a technique within a therapy session.

Anxiety

Anxiety is a psychological and physiological state characterized by somatic, emotional, cognitive, and behavioral components. The root meaning of the word anxiety is 'to vex or trouble'; in either the absence or presence of psychological stress, anxiety can create feelings of fear, worry, uneasiness and dread. Anxiety is considered to be a normal reaction to stress.

Anxiety disorder

Anxiety disorders are blanket terms covering several different forms of abnormal and pathological fear and anxiety which only came under the aegis of psychiatry at the very end of the 19th century. Gelder, Mayou ' Geddes (2005) explains that anxiety disorders are classified in two groups: continuous symptoms and episodic symptoms. Current psychiatric diagnostic criteria recognize a wide variety of anxiety disorders.

Attention deficit hyperactivity disorder

Attention deficit hyperactivity disorder is a neurobehavioral developmental disorder. It is primarily characterized by "the co-existence of attentional problems and hyperactivity, with each behavior occurring infrequently alone" and symptoms starting before seven years of age.

	Attention deficit hyperactivity disorder is the most commonly studied and diagnosed psychiatric disorder in children, affecting about 3 to 5 percent of children globally and diagnosed in about 2 to 16 percent of school aged children.
Generalized anxiety disorder	Generalized anxiety disorder is an anxiety disorder that is characterized by excessive, uncontrollable and often irrational worry about everyday things that is disproportionate to the actual source of worry. This excessive worry often interferes with daily functioning, as individuals suffering Generalized anxiety disorder typically anticipate disaster, and are overly concerned about everyday matters such as health issues, money, death, family problems, friend problems, relationship problems or work difficulties. They often exhibit a variety of physical symptoms, including fatigue, fidgeting, headaches, nausea, numbness in hands and feet, muscle tension, muscle aches, difficulty swallowing, bouts of difficulty breathing, difficulty concentrating, trembling, twitching, irritability, agitation, sweating, restlessness, insomnia, hot flashes, and rashes and inability to fully control the anxiety.
Hyperactivity	Hyperactivity can be described as a physical state in which a person is abnormally and easily excitable or exuberant. Strong emotional reactions, impulsive behavior, and sometimes a short span of attention are also typical for a hyperactive person. Some individuals may show these characteristics naturally, as personality differs from person to person.
Mental health	Mental health describes either a level of cognitive or emotional well-being or an absence of a mental disorder. From perspectives of the discipline of positive psychology or holism mental health may include an individual's ability to enjoy life and procure a balance between life activities and efforts to achieve psychological resilience. Mental health is an expression of our emotions and signifies a successful adaptation to a range of demands.
Psychosis	Psychosis means abnormal condition of the mind, and is a generic psychiatric term for a mental state often described as involving a "loss of contact with reality". People suffering from psychosis are described as psychotic. Psychosis is given to the more severe forms of psychiatric disorder, during which hallucinations and delusions and impaired insight may occur.
Experience	Experience as a general concept comprises knowledge of or skill in or observation of some thing or some event gained through involvement in or exposure to that thing or event. The history of the word experience aligns it closely with the concept of experiment.

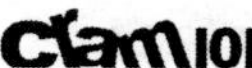

The concept of experience generally refers to know-how or procedural knowledge, rather than propositional knowledge: on-the-job training rather than book-learning.

Infertility	Infertility primarily refers to the biological inability of a person to contribute to conception. Infertility may also refer to the state of a woman who is unable to carry a pregnancy to full term. There are many biological causes of infertility, some which may be bypassed with medical intervention. Women who are fertile experience a natural period of fertility before and during ovulation, and they are naturally infertile during the rest of the menstrual cycle. Fertility awareness methods are used to discern when these changes occur by tracking changes in cervical mucus or basal body temperature.
Motivation	Motivation is the driving force which causes us to achieve goals. Motivation is said to be intrinsic or extrinsic. The term is generally used for humans but, theoretically, it can also be used to describe the causes for animal behavior as well.
Reuptake	Reuptake is the reabsorption of a neurotransmitter by a neurotransmitter transporter of a pre-synaptic neuron after it has performed its function of transmitting a neural impulse. Reuptake is necessary for normal synaptic physiology because it allows for the recycling of neurotransmitters and regulates the level of neurotransmitter present in the synapse and controls how long a signal resulting from neurotransmitter release lasts. Because neurotransmitters are too large and hydrophilic to diffuse through the membrane, specific transport proteins are necessary for the reabsorption of neurotransmitters. Much research, both biochemical and structural, has been performed to obtain clues about the mechanism of reuptake.
Selective serotonin reuptake inhibitor	Selective serotonin reuptake inhibitors or serotonin-specific reuptake inhibitor are a class of compounds typically used as antidepressants in the treatment of depression, anxiety disorders, and some personality disorders. They are also typically effective and used in treating some cases of insomnia.

	Selective serotonin reuptake inhibitors are believed to increase the extracellular level of the neurotransmitter serotonin by inhibiting its reuptake into the presynaptic cell, increasing the level of serotonin in the synaptic cleft available to bind to the postsynaptic receptor.
Serotonin	Serotonin is a monoamine neurotransmitter. Biochemically derived from tryptophan, serotonin is primarily found in the gastrointestinal (GI) tract, platelets, and in the central nervous system (CNS) of animals including humans. It is a well-known contributor to feelings of well-being; therefore it is also known as a "happiness hormone" despite not being a hormone.
Cognitive development	Cognitive development is a field of study in neuroscience and psychology focusing on a child's development in terms of information processing, conceptual resources, perceptual skill, language learning, and other aspects of brain development and cognitive psychology. A large portion of research has gone into understanding how a child conceptualizes the world. Jean Piaget was a major force in the founding of this field, forming his "theory of cognitive development".
Social environment	The social environment of an individual is the culture that s/he was educated and/or lives in, and the people and institutions with whom the person interacts. The interaction may be in person or through communication media, even anonymous or one-way, and may not imply equality of social status. Therefore the social environment is a broader concept than that of social class or social circle. Nevertheless, persons with the same social environment often develop a sense of solidarity; they often tend to trust and help one another, and to congregate in social groups. They will often think in similar styles and patterns even when their conclusions differ.

Anxiety	Anxiety is a psychological and physiological state characterized by somatic, emotional, cognitive, and behavioral components. The root meaning of the word anxiety is 'to vex or trouble'; in either the absence or presence of psychological stress, anxiety can create feelings of fear, worry, uneasiness and dread. Anxiety is considered to be a normal reaction to stress.
Anxiety disorder	Anxiety disorders are blanket terms covering several different forms of abnormal and pathological fear and anxiety which only came under the aegis of psychiatry at the very end of the 19th century. Gelder, Mayou ' Geddes (2005) explains that anxiety disorders are classified in two groups: continuous symptoms and episodic symptoms. Current psychiatric diagnostic criteria recognize a wide variety of anxiety disorders.
Generalized anxiety disorder	Generalized anxiety disorder is an anxiety disorder that is characterized by excessive, uncontrollable and often irrational worry about everyday things that is disproportionate to the actual source of worry. This excessive worry often interferes with daily functioning, as individuals suffering Generalized anxiety disorder typically anticipate disaster, and are overly concerned about everyday matters such as health issues, money, death, family problems, friend problems, relationship problems or work difficulties. They often exhibit a variety of physical symptoms, including fatigue, fidgeting, headaches, nausea, numbness in hands and feet, muscle tension, muscle aches, difficulty swallowing, bouts of difficulty breathing, difficulty concentrating, trembling, twitching, irritability, agitation, sweating, restlessness, insomnia, hot flashes, and rashes and inability to fully control the anxiety.
Glucocorticoid	Glucocorticoids are a class of steroid hormones that bind to the glucocorticoid receptor (GR), which is present in almost every vertebrate animal cell. Glucocorticoids are part of the feedback mechanism in the immune system that turns immune activity (inflammation) down. They are therefore used in medicine to treat diseases that are caused by an overactive immune system, such as allergies, asthma, autoimmune diseases and sepsis. Glucocorticoids have many diverse (pleiotropic) effects, including potentially harmful side effects, and as a result are rarely sold over-the-counter. They also interfere with some of the abnormal mechanisms in cancer cells, so they are used in high doses to treat cancer.
Infertility	Infertility primarily refers to the biological inability of a person to contribute to conception. Infertility may also refer to the state of a woman who is unable to carry a pregnancy to full term. There are many biological causes of infertility, some which may be bypassed with medical intervention.

Women who are fertile experience a natural period of fertility before and during ovulation, and they are naturally infertile during the rest of the menstrual cycle. Fertility awareness methods are used to discern when these changes occur by tracking changes in cervical mucus or basal body temperature.

Reuptake	Reuptake is the reabsorption of a neurotransmitter by a neurotransmitter transporter of a pre-synaptic neuron after it has performed its function of transmitting a neural impulse. Reuptake is necessary for normal synaptic physiology because it allows for the recycling of neurotransmitters and regulates the level of neurotransmitter present in the synapse and controls how long a signal resulting from neurotransmitter release lasts. Because neurotransmitters are too large and hydrophilic to diffuse through the membrane, specific transport proteins are necessary for the reabsorption of neurotransmitters. Much research, both biochemical and structural, has been performed to obtain clues about the mechanism of reuptake.
Selective serotonin reuptake inhibitor	Selective serotonin reuptake inhibitors or serotonin-specific reuptake inhibitor are a class of compounds typically used as antidepressants in the treatment of depression, anxiety disorders, and some personality disorders. They are also typically effective and used in treating some cases of insomnia. Selective serotonin reuptake inhibitors are believed to increase the extracellular level of the neurotransmitter serotonin by inhibiting its reuptake into the presynaptic cell, increasing the level of serotonin in the synaptic cleft available to bind to the postsynaptic receptor.
Serotonin	Serotonin is a monoamine neurotransmitter. Biochemically derived from tryptophan, serotonin is primarily found in the gastrointestinal (GI) tract, platelets, and in the central nervous system (CNS) of animals including humans. It is a well-known contributor to feelings of well-being; therefore it is also known as a "happiness hormone" despite not being a hormone.
Infant	An infant is the very young offspring of humans. A newborn is an infant who is within hours, days, or up to a few weeks from birth. In medical contexts, newborn or neonate refers to an infant in the first 28 days of life (from birth up to 4 weeks after birth, less than a month old).

Beck Depression Inventory

The Beck Depression Inventory created by Dr. Aaron T. Beck, is a 21-question multiple-choice self-report inventory, one of the most widely used instruments for measuring the severity of depression. Its development marked a shift among health care professionals, who had until then viewed depression from a psychodynamic perspective, instead of it being rooted in the patient's own thoughts.

In its current version the questionnaire is designed for individuals aged 13 and over, and is composed of items relating to symptoms of depression such as hopelessness and irritability, cognitions such as guilt or feelings of being punished, as well as physical symptoms such as fatigue, weight loss, and lack of interest in sex.

Depression

Depression is a state of low mood and aversion to activity that can affect a person's thoughts, behaviour, feelings and physical well-being. It may include feelings of sadness, anxiety, emptiness, hopelessness, worthlessness, guilt, irritability, or restlessness. Depressed people may lose interest in activities that once were pleasurable, experience difficulty concentrating, remembering details, or making decisions, and may contemplate or attempt suicide.

Animal studies

Animal studies is a recently recognized field in which animals are studied in a variety of cross-disciplinary ways. Scholars from fields as diverse as: art history, anthropology, biology, film studies, geography, history, psychology, literary studies, museology, philosophy, and sociology; and from various theoretical perspectives, including: feminism, marxist theory, and queer theory, seek to understand both human-animal relations now and in the past, and to understand animals as beings-in-themselves separate from our knowledge of them. Because the field is still developing, scholars and others have some freedom to define their own criteria and structure for the field.

Attention deficit hyperactivity disorder

Attention deficit hyperactivity disorder is a neurobehavioral developmental disorder. It is primarily characterized by "the co-existence of attentional problems and hyperactivity, with each behavior occurring infrequently alone" and symptoms starting before seven years of age.

Attention deficit hyperactivity disorder is the most commonly studied and diagnosed psychiatric disorder in children, affecting about 3 to 5 percent of children globally and diagnosed in about 2 to 16 percent of school aged children.

Benzodiazepine	A benzodiazepine is a psychoactive drug whose core chemical structure is the fusion of a benzene ring and a diazepine ring. The first benzodiazepine, chlordiazepoxide (Librium), was discovered accidentally by Leo Sternbach in 1955, and made available in 1960 by Hoffmann-La Roche, which has also marketed diazepam (Valium) since 1963.
Carbohydrate metabolism	Carbohydrate metabolism denotes the various biochemical processes responsible for the formation, breakdown and interconversion of carbohydrates in living organisms. The most important carbohydrate is glucose, a simple sugar (monosaccharide) that is metabolized by nearly all known organisms. Glucose and other carbohydrates are part of a wide variety of metabolic pathways across species: plants synthesize carbohydrates from atmospheric gases by photosynthesis storing the absorbed energy internally, often in the form of starch or lipids.
Hyperactivity	Hyperactivity can be described as a physical state in which a person is abnormally and easily excitable or exuberant. Strong emotional reactions, impulsive behavior, and sometimes a short span of attention are also typical for a hyperactive person. Some individuals may show these characteristics naturally, as personality differs from person to person.
Hypnotic	Hypnotic drugs are a class of psychoactives whose primary function is to induce sleep and to be used in the treatment of insomnia and in surgical anesthesia. When used in anesthesia to produce and maintain unconsciousness, "sleep" is metaphorical and there are no regular sleep stages or cyclical natural states; patients rarely recover from anesthesia feeling refreshed and with renewed energy. Because drugs in this class generally produce dose-dependent effects, ranging from anxiolysis to production of unconsciousness, they are often referred to collectively as sedative-hypnotic drugs.
Prenatal stress	Prenatal stress is exposure of an expectant mother to distress, which can be caused by stressful life events or by environmental hardships. The resulting changes to the mother's hormonal and immune system may harm the fetus's (and after birth, the infant's) immune function and brain development.
Alcohol Use Disorders Identification Test	The Alcohol Use Disorders Identification Test is a simple ten-question test developed by the World Health Organization to determine if a person's alcohol consumption may be harmful. The test was designed to be used internationally, and was validated in a study using patients from six countries. Questions 1-3 deal with alcohol consumption, 4-6 relate to alcohol dependence and 7-10 consider alcohol related problems.

Identification	Identification is a psychological process whereby the subject assimilates an aspect, property, or attribute of the other and is transformed, wholly or partially, after the model the other provides. It is by means of a series of identifications that the personality is constituted and specified. The roots of the concept can be found in Freud's writings.
Fetal alcohol syndrome	Fetal/Foetal alcohol syndrome is a pattern of mental and physical defects that can develop in a fetus when a woman drinks alcohol during pregnancy. The timing and frequency of alcohol consumption during pregnancy are major factors in the risk of a child developing fetal alcohol syndrome. While the ingestion of alcohol does not always result in Fetal alcohol syndrome, there are no medically established guidelines for safe levels of alcohol consumption during pregnancy.
Nicotine	Nicotine is an alkaloid found in the nightshade family of plants (Solanaceae) that constitutes approximately 0.6-3.0% of the dry weight of tobacco, with biosynthesis taking place in the roots and accumulation occurring in the leaves. It functions as an antiherbivore chemical with particular specificity to insects; therefore nicotine was widely used as an insecticide in the past, and currently nicotine analogs such as imidacloprid continue to be widely used. Nicotine is also found in several other members of the Solanaceae family, with small amounts being present in species such as the eggplant and tomato.
Norepinephrine	Norepinephrine is a catecholamine with multiple roles including as a hormone and a neurotransmitter. As a stress hormone, norepinephrine affects parts of the brain, such as the amygdala, where attention and responses are controlled. Along with epinephrine, norepinephrine also underlies the fight-or-flight response, directly increasing heart rate, triggering the release of glucose from energy stores, and increasing blood flow to skeletal muscle. It increases the brain's oxygen supply. Norepinephrine can also suppress neuroinflammation when released diffusely in the brain from the locus ceruleus.
Smoking	Smoking is a practice in which a substance, most commonly tobacco or cannabis, is burned and the smoke is tasted or inhaled. This is primarily practised as a route of administration for recreational drug use, as combustion releases the active substances in drugs such as nicotine and makes them available for absorption through the lungs. It can also be done as a part of rituals, to induce trances and spiritual enlightenment.

Child development	Child development refers to the biological and psychological changes that occur in human beings between birth and the end of adolescence, as the individual progresses from dependency to increasing autonomy. Because these developmental changes may be strongly influenced by genetic factors and events during prenatal life, genetics and prenatal development are usually included as part of the study of child development. Related terms include developmental psychology, referring to development throughout the lifespan, and pediatrics, the branch of medicine relating to the care of children. Developmental change may occur as a result of genetically-controlled processes known as maturation, or as a result of environmental factors and learning, but most commonly involves an interaction between the two.
Social exclusion	Social exclusion is a multidimensional process of progressive social rupture, detaching groups and individuals from social relations and institutions and preventing them from full participation in the normal, normatively prescribed activities of the society in which they live. Another definition of this sociological term is as follows: The outcome of multiple deprivations that prevent individuals or groups from participating fully in the economic, social, and political life of the society in which they live. An inherent problem with the term, however, is the tendency of its use by practitioners who define it to fit their argument.
Contingency management	Contingency management is a type of treatment used in the mental health or substance abuse fields. Patients are rewarded (or, less often, punished) for their behavior; generally, adherence to or failure to adhere to program rules and regulations or their treatment plan. For children with conduct disorder, token systems are highly successful but do not help the children achieve normal functioning unless combined with a cost response program reinforcing negative punishment.

Relaxation technique	A relaxation technique is any method, process, procedure, or activity that helps a person to relax; to attain a state of increased calmness; or otherwise reduce levels of anxiety, stress or anger. Relaxation techniques are often employed as one element of a wider stress management program and can decrease muscle tension, lower the blood pressure and slow heart and breath rates, among other health benefits. Since the 1960s, research has indicated strong correlations between chronic stress and physical and emotional health.
Envy	Envy is best defined as an emotion that "occurs when a person lacks another's (perceived) superior quality, achievement, or possession and either desires it or wishes that the other lacked it." Envy can also derive from a sense of low self-esteem that results from an upward social comparison threatening a person's self image: another person has something that the envier considers to be important to have. If the other person is perceived to be similar to the envier, the aroused envy will be particularly intense, because it signals to the envier that it just as well could have been he or she who had the desired object. Bertrand Russell said envy was one of the most potent causes of unhappiness.
Penis envy	Penis envy in Freudian psychoanalysis refers to the theorized reaction of a girl during her psychosexual development to the realization that she does not have a penis. Freud considered this realization a defining moment in the development of gender and sexual identity for women. According to Freud, the parallel reaction in boys to the realization that girls do not have a penis is castration anxiety.

Denial

Denial is a defense mechanism postulated by Sigmund Freud, in which a person is faced with a fact that is too uncomfortable to accept and rejects it instead, insisting that it is not true despite what may be overwhelming evidence. The subject may use:

- simple denial - deny the reality of the unpleasant fact altogether
- minimisation - admit the fact but deny its seriousness (a combination of denial and rationalisation), or
- projection - admit both the fact and seriousness but deny responsibility.

The concept of denial is particularly important to the study of addiction. The theory of denial was first researched seriously by Anna Freud.

Incest

Incest is sexual intercourse between close relatives that is illegal in the jurisdiction where it takes place and/or is socially taboo. The type of sexual activity and the nature of the relationship between people that constitutes a breach of law or social taboo vary with culture and jurisdiction. Some societies consider incest to include only those who live in the same household, or who belong to the same clan or lineage; other societies consider it to include "blood relatives"; other societies further include those related by adoption or marriage.

Capacity

The capacity of both natural and legal persons determines whether they may make binding amendments to their rights, duties and obligations, such as getting married or merging, entering into contracts, making gifts, or writing a valid will. Capacity is an aspect of status and both are defined by a person's personal law:

- for natural persons, the law of domicile or lex domicilii in common law jurisdictions, and either the law of nationality or lex patriae, or of habitual residence in civil law states;
- for legal persons, the law of the place of incorporation, the lex incorporationis for companies while other forms of business entity derive their capacity either from the law of the place in which they were formed or the laws of the states in which they establish a presence for trading purposes depending on the nature of the entity and the transactions entered into.

When the law limits or bars a person from engaging in specified activities, any agreements or contracts to do so are either voidable or void for incapacity. Sometimes such legal incapacity is referred to as incompetence.

Intervention

An intervention is an orchestrated attempt by one, or often many, people (usually family and friends) to get someone to seek professional help with an addiction or some kind of traumatic event or crisis, or other serious problem. The term intervention is most often used when the traumatic event involves addiction to drugs or other items. Intervention can also refer to the act of using a technique within a therapy session.

Mental health

Mental health describes either a level of cognitive or emotional well-being or an absence of a mental disorder. From perspectives of the discipline of positive psychology or holism mental health may include an individual's ability to enjoy life and procure a balance between life activities and efforts to achieve psychological resilience. Mental health is an expression of our emotions and signifies a successful adaptation to a range of demands.

Pedophilia

As a medical diagnosis, pedophilia is typically defined as a psychiatric disorder in adults or late adolescents (persons age 16 and older) characterized by a primary or exclusive sexual interest in prepubescent children (generally age 13 years or younger, though onset of puberty may vary). The child must be at least five years younger in the case of adolescent pedophiles. The word comes from the Greek: πα?ς (paîs), meaning "child," and φιλ?α (philía), "friendly love" or "friendship", though this literal meaning has been altered toward sexual attraction in modern times, under the titles "child love" or "child lover", by pedophiles who use symbols and codes to identify their preferences.

Borderline personality disorder

Borderline personality disorder is a personality disorder described as a prolonged disturbance of personality function in a person (generally over the age of eighteen years, although it is also found in adolescents), characterized by depth and variability of moods. The disorder typically involves unusual levels of instability in mood; black and white thinking, or splitting; the disorder often manifests itself in idealization and devaluation episodes, as well as chaotic and unstable interpersonal relationships, self-image, identity, and behavior; as well as a disturbance in the individual's sense of self. In extreme cases, this disturbance in the sense of self can lead to periods of dissociation.

Abortion	Abortion is the termination of a pregnancy by the removal or expulsion of a fetus or embryo from the uterus, resulting in or caused by its death. An abortion can occur spontaneously due to complications during pregnancy or can be induced, in humans and other species. In the context of human pregnancies, an abortion induced to preserve the health of the gravida (pregnant female) is termed a therapeutic abortion, while an abortion induced for any other reason is termed an elective abortion.
Tokophobia	Tokophobia, is a form of specific phobia.
Schizophrenia	Schizophrenia is a mental disorder characterized by a disintegration of thought processes and of emotional responsiveness. It most commonly manifests as auditory hallucinations, paranoid or bizarre delusions, or disorganized speech and thinking, and it is accompanied by significant social or occupational dysfunction. The onset of symptoms typically occurs in young adulthood, with a global lifetime prevalence of about 0.3-0.7%.
Bipolar disorder	Bipolar disorder, also referred to as bipolar affective disorder or manic depression, is a psychiatric diagnosis that describes a category of mood disorders defined by the presence of one or more episodes of abnormally elevated energy levels, cognition, and mood with or without one or more depressive episodes. The elevated moods are clinically referred to as mania or, if milder, hypomania. Individuals who experience manic episodes also commonly experience depressive episodes, or symptoms, or mixed episodes in which features of both mania and depression are present at the same time.
Mental disorder	A mental disorder is a psychological or behavioral pattern generally associated with subjective distress or disability that occurs in an individual, and which is not a part of normal development or culture. The recognition and understanding of mental health conditions has changed over time and across cultures, and there are still variations in the definition, assessment, and classification of mental disorders, although standard guideline criteria are widely accepted. A few mental disorders are diagnosed based on the harm to others, regardless of the subject's perception of distress.
Pain	Pain is "an unpleasant sensory and emotional experience associated with actual or potential tissue damage, or described in terms of such damage." It is the feeling common to such experiences as stubbing a toe, burning a finger, putting iodine on a cut, and bumping the "funny bone".

Pain motivates us to withdraw from potentially damaging situations, protect a damaged body part while it heals, and avoid those situations in the future. Most pain resolves promptly once the painful stimulus is removed and the body has healed, but sometimes pain persists despite removal of the stimulus and apparent healing of the body; and sometimes pain arises in the absence of any detectable stimulus, damage or disease.

Panic disorder

Panic disorder is an anxiety disorder characterized by recurring severe panic attacks. It may also include significant behavioral change lasting at least a month and of ongoing worry about the implications or concern about having other attacks. The latter are called anticipatory attacks (DSM-IVR).

Anorexia nervosa

Anorexia nervosa is an eating disorder characterized by refusal to maintain a healthy body weight and an obsessive fear of gaining weight. It is often coupled with a distorted self image which may be maintained by various cognitive biases that alter how the affected individual evaluates and thinks about her or his body, food and eating. Persons with anorexia nervosa continue to feel hunger, but deny themselves all but very small quantities of food.

Eating disorder

Eating disorders refer to a group of conditions characterized by abnormal eating habits that may involve either insufficient or excessive food intake to the detriment of an individual's physical and mental health. Binge eating disorder, bulimia nervosa, anorexia nervosa being the most common specific forms in the United States. Though primarily thought of as affecting females (an estimated 5-10 million being affected in the U.S)., eating disorders affect males as well (an estimated 1 million U.S. males being affected).

Personality disorder

Personality disorders, formerly referred to as character disorders, are a class of personality types and behaviors that the American Psychiatric Association (APA) defines as "an enduring pattern of inner experience and behavior that deviates markedly from the expectations of the culture of the individual who exhibits it". Personality disorders are noted on Axis II of the Diagnostic and Statistical Manual of Mental Disorders or DSM-IV-TR (fourth edition, text revision) of the American Psychiatric Association.

Motivational interviewing

Motivational interviewing refers to a counseling approach in part developed by clinical psychologists Professor William R Miller, Ph.D. and Professor Stephen Rollnick, Ph.D. It is a client-centered, semi-directive method of engaging intrinsic motivation to change behavior by developing discrepancy and exploring and resolving ambivalence within the client.

	Motivational interviewing recognizes and accepts the fact that clients who need to make changes in their lives approach counseling at different levels of readiness to change their behavior. If the counseling is mandated, they may never have thought of changing the behavior in question.
Self-esteem	Self-esteem is a term used in psychology to reflect a person's overall evaluation or appraisal of his or her own worth. Self-esteem encompasses beliefs (for example, "I am competent", "I am worthy") and emotions such as triumph, despair, pride and shame. Self-esteem can apply specifically to a particular dimension (for example, "I believe I am a good writer and I feel proud about that") or have global extent (for example, "I believe I am a bad person, and feel bad of myself in general").
Self-harm	Self-harm or deliberate self-harm includes self-injury (SI) and self-poisoning and is defined as the intentional, direct injuring of body tissue without suicidal intent. These terms are used in the more recent literature in an attempt to reach a more neutral terminology. The older literature, especially that which predates the DSM-IV-TR, almost exclusively refers to self-mutilation.
Intrusive thoughts	Intrusive thoughts are unwelcome involuntary thoughts, images, or unpleasant ideas that may become obsessions, are upsetting or distressing, and can be difficult to manage or eliminate. Most people experience these thoughts when they are associated with obsessive-compulsive disorder (OCD), depression, and sometimes attention-deficit hyperactive disorder (ADHD). They may become paralyzing, anxiety-provoking, or persistent.
Quality of life	The term quality of life is used to evaluate the general well-being of individuals and societies. The term is used in a wide range of contexts, including the fields of international development, healthcare, and politics. Quality of life should not be confused with the concept of standard of living, which is based primarily on income.
Mental retardation	Mental retardation is a generalized disorder appearing before adulthood, characterized by significantly impaired cognitive functioning and deficits in two or more adaptive behaviors. It has historically been defined as an Intelligence Quotient score under 70. Once focused almost entirely on cognition, the definition now includes both a component relating to mental functioning and one relating to individuals' functional skills in their environment. As a result, a person with a below-average intelligence quotient (BAIQ) may not be considered mentally retarded.

Representation	Representation is a term used in cognitive psychology, neuroscience, and cognitive science to refer to a hypothetical internal cognitive symbol that represents external reality. David Marr defines representation as "a formal system for making explicit certain entities or types of information, together with a specification of how the system does this." Representationalism (also known as indirect realism) is the view that representations are the main way we access external reality.
Ambivalence	Ambivalence is a state of having simultaneous, conflicting feelings toward a person or thing. Stated another way, ambivalence is the experience of having thoughts and emotions of both positive and negative valence toward someone or something. A common example of ambivalence is the feeling of both love and hate for a person.

Mental disorder	A mental disorder is a psychological or behavioral pattern generally associated with subjective distress or disability that occurs in an individual, and which is not a part of normal development or culture. The recognition and understanding of mental health conditions has changed over time and across cultures, and there are still variations in the definition, assessment, and classification of mental disorders, although standard guideline criteria are widely accepted. A few mental disorders are diagnosed based on the harm to others, regardless of the subject's perception of distress.
Representation	Representation is a term used in cognitive psychology, neuroscience, and cognitive science to refer to a hypothetical internal cognitive symbol that represents external reality. David Marr defines representation as "a formal system for making explicit certain entities or types of information, together with a specification of how the system does this." Representationalism (also known as indirect realism) is the view that representations are the main way we access external reality.
Infant	An infant is the very young offspring of humans. A newborn is an infant who is within hours, days, or up to a few weeks from birth. In medical contexts, newborn or neonate refers to an infant in the first 28 days of life (from birth up to 4 weeks after birth, less than a month old).
Perception	In philosophy, psychology, and cognitive science, perception is the process of attaining awareness or understanding of sensory information. The word "perception" comes from the Latin words perceptio, percipio, and means "receiving, collecting, action of taking possession, apprehension with the mind or senses." Perception is one of the oldest fields in psychology. The oldest quantitative law in psychology is the Weber-Fechner law, which quantifies the relationship between the intensity of physical stimuli and their perceptual effects (for example, testing how much darker a computer screen can get before the viewer actually notices).
Depression	Depression is a state of low mood and aversion to activity that can affect a person's thoughts, behaviour, feelings and physical well-being. It may include feelings of sadness, anxiety, emptiness, hopelessness, worthlessness, guilt, irritability, or restlessness. Depressed people may lose interest in activities that once were pleasurable, experience difficulty concentrating, remembering details, or making decisions, and may contemplate or attempt suicide.

Monoamine oxidase inhibitor	Monoamine oxidase inhibitors (MAOIs) are a class of antidepressant drugs prescribed for the treatment of depression. They are particularly effective in treating atypical depression. Because of potentially lethal dietary and drug interactions, monoamine oxidase inhibitors have historically been reserved as a last line of treatment, used only when other classes of antidepressant drugs (for example selective serotonin reuptake inhibitors and tricyclic antidepressants) have failed.
Ambivalence	Ambivalence is a state of having simultaneous, conflicting feelings toward a person or thing. Stated another way, ambivalence is the experience of having thoughts and emotions of both positive and negative valence toward someone or something. A common example of ambivalence is the feeling of both love and hate for a person.
Contingency management	Contingency management is a type of treatment used in the mental health or substance abuse fields. Patients are rewarded (or, less often, punished) for their behavior; generally, adherence to or failure to adhere to program rules and regulations or their treatment plan. For children with conduct disorder, token systems are highly successful but do not help the children achieve normal functioning unless combined with a cost response program reinforcing negative punishment.
Alcohol Use Disorders Identification Test	The Alcohol Use Disorders Identification Test is a simple ten-question test developed by the World Health Organization to determine if a person's alcohol consumption may be harmful. The test was designed to be used internationally, and was validated in a study using patients from six countries. Questions 1-3 deal with alcohol consumption, 4-6 relate to alcohol dependence and 7-10 consider alcohol related problems.
Identification	Identification is a psychological process whereby the subject assimilates an aspect, property, or attribute of the other and is transformed, wholly or partially, after the model the other provides. It is by means of a series of identifications that the personality is constituted and specified. The roots of the concept can be found in Freud's writings.
Paradigm	The word paradigm has been used in science to describe distinct concepts. It comes from Greek "παρ?δειγμα" (paradeigma), "pattern, example, sample" from the verb "παραδε?κνυμι" (paradeiknumi), "exhibit, represent, expose" and that from "παρ?" (para), "beside, by" + "δε?κνυμι" (deiknumi), "to show, to point out".

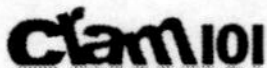

The original Greek term παραδε?γματι (paradeigma) was used in Greek texts such as Plato's Timaeus (28A) as the model or the pattern that the Demiurge (god) used to create the cosmos.

Chapter 5. Treatment of abnormal states during pregnancy

Intervention	An intervention is an orchestrated attempt by one, or often many, people (usually family and friends) to get someone to seek professional help with an addiction or some kind of traumatic event or crisis, or other serious problem. The term intervention is most often used when the traumatic event involves addiction to drugs or other items. Intervention can also refer to the act of using a technique within a therapy session.
Anxiety	Anxiety is a psychological and physiological state characterized by somatic, emotional, cognitive, and behavioral components. The root meaning of the word anxiety is 'to vex or trouble'; in either the absence or presence of psychological stress, anxiety can create feelings of fear, worry, uneasiness and dread. Anxiety is considered to be a normal reaction to stress.
Depression	Depression is a state of low mood and aversion to activity that can affect a person's thoughts, behaviour, feelings and physical well-being. It may include feelings of sadness, anxiety, emptiness, hopelessness, worthlessness, guilt, irritability, or restlessness. Depressed people may lose interest in activities that once were pleasurable, experience difficulty concentrating, remembering details, or making decisions, and may contemplate or attempt suicide.
Mental disorder	A mental disorder is a psychological or behavioral pattern generally associated with subjective distress or disability that occurs in an individual, and which is not a part of normal development or culture. The recognition and understanding of mental health conditions has changed over time and across cultures, and there are still variations in the definition, assessment, and classification of mental disorders, although standard guideline criteria are widely accepted. A few mental disorders are diagnosed based on the harm to others, regardless of the subject's perception of distress.
Abortion	Abortion is the termination of a pregnancy by the removal or expulsion of a fetus or embryo from the uterus, resulting in or caused by its death. An abortion can occur spontaneously due to complications during pregnancy or can be induced, in humans and other species. In the context of human pregnancies, an abortion induced to preserve the health of the gravida (pregnant female) is termed a therapeutic abortion, while an abortion induced for any other reason is termed an elective abortion.
Antidepressant	An antidepressant is a psychiatric medication used to alleviate mood disorders, such as major depression and dysthymia and anxiety disorders such as social anxiety disorder. According to Gelder, Mayou '*Geddes (2005) people with a depressive illness will experience a therapeutic effect to their mood, however this will not be experienced in healthy individuals. Drugs including the monoamine oxidase inhibitors (MAOIs), tricyclic antidepressants (TCAs), tetracyclic antidepressants (TeCAs), selective serotonin reuptake inhibitors (SSRIs), and serotonin-norepinephrine reuptake inhibitors (SNRIs) are most commonly associated with the term.

Chapter 5. Treatment of abnormal states during pregnancy

Infertility	Infertility primarily refers to the biological inability of a person to contribute to conception. Infertility may also refer to the state of a woman who is unable to carry a pregnancy to full term. There are many biological causes of infertility, some which may be bypassed with medical intervention. Women who are fertile experience a natural period of fertility before and during ovulation, and they are naturally infertile during the rest of the menstrual cycle. Fertility awareness methods are used to discern when these changes occur by tracking changes in cervical mucus or basal body temperature.
Nicotine	Nicotine is an alkaloid found in the nightshade family of plants (Solanaceae) that constitutes approximately 0.6-3.0% of the dry weight of tobacco, with biosynthesis taking place in the roots and accumulation occurring in the leaves. It functions as an antiherbivore chemical with particular specificity to insects; therefore nicotine was widely used as an insecticide in the past, and currently nicotine analogs such as imidacloprid continue to be widely used. Nicotine is also found in several other members of the Solanaceae family, with small amounts being present in species such as the eggplant and tomato.
Reuptake	Reuptake is the reabsorption of a neurotransmitter by a neurotransmitter transporter of a pre-synaptic neuron after it has performed its function of transmitting a neural impulse. Reuptake is necessary for normal synaptic physiology because it allows for the recycling of neurotransmitters and regulates the level of neurotransmitter present in the synapse and controls how long a signal resulting from neurotransmitter release lasts. Because neurotransmitters are too large and hydrophilic to diffuse through the membrane, specific transport proteins are necessary for the reabsorption of neurotransmitters. Much research, both biochemical and structural, has been performed to obtain clues about the mechanism of reuptake.
Selective serotonin reuptake inhibitor	Selective serotonin reuptake inhibitors or serotonin-specific reuptake inhibitor are a class of compounds typically used as antidepressants in the treatment of depression, anxiety disorders, and some personality disorders. They are also typically effective and used in treating some cases of insomnia. Selective serotonin reuptake inhibitors are believed to increase the extracellular level of the neurotransmitter serotonin by inhibiting its reuptake into the presynaptic cell, increasing the level of serotonin in the synaptic cleft available to bind to the postsynaptic receptor.

Chapter 5. Treatment of abnormal states during pregnancy

Serotonin	Serotonin is a monoamine neurotransmitter. Biochemically derived from tryptophan, serotonin is primarily found in the gastrointestinal (GI) tract, platelets, and in the central nervous system (CNS) of animals including humans. It is a well-known contributor to feelings of well-being; therefore it is also known as a "happiness hormone" despite not being a hormone.
Smoking	Smoking is a practice in which a substance, most commonly tobacco or cannabis, is burned and the smoke is tasted or inhaled. This is primarily practised as a route of administration for recreational drug use, as combustion releases the active substances in drugs such as nicotine and makes them available for absorption through the lungs. It can also be done as a part of rituals, to induce trances and spiritual enlightenment.
Monoamine oxidase inhibitor	Monoamine oxidase inhibitors (MAOIs) are a class of antidepressant drugs prescribed for the treatment of depression. They are particularly effective in treating atypical depression. Because of potentially lethal dietary and drug interactions, monoamine oxidase inhibitors have historically been reserved as a last line of treatment, used only when other classes of antidepressant drugs (for example selective serotonin reuptake inhibitors and tricyclic antidepressants) have failed.
Beck Depression Inventory	The Beck Depression Inventory created by Dr. Aaron T. Beck, is a 21-question multiple-choice self-report inventory, one of the most widely used instruments for measuring the severity of depression. Its development marked a shift among health care professionals, who had until then viewed depression from a psychodynamic perspective, instead of it being rooted in the patient's own thoughts. In its current version the questionnaire is designed for individuals aged 13 and over, and is composed of items relating to symptoms of depression such as hopelessness and irritability, cognitions such as guilt or feelings of being punished, as well as physical symptoms such as fatigue, weight loss, and lack of interest in sex.
Anxiolytic	An anxiolytic is a drug used for the treatment of anxiety, and its related psychological and physical symptoms. Anxiolytics have been shown to be useful in the treatment of anxiety disorders.

Beta-receptor blockers such as propranolol and oxprenolol, although not anxiolytics, can be used to combat the somatic symptoms of anxiety.

Benzodiazepine

A benzodiazepine is a psychoactive drug whose core chemical structure is the fusion of a benzene ring and a diazepine ring. The first benzodiazepine, chlordiazepoxide (Librium), was discovered accidentally by Leo Sternbach in 1955, and made available in 1960 by Hoffmann-La Roche, which has also marketed diazepam (Valium) since 1963.

Infant

An infant is the very young offspring of humans. A newborn is an infant who is within hours, days, or up to a few weeks from birth. In medical contexts, newborn or neonate refers to an infant in the first 28 days of life (from birth up to 4 weeks after birth, less than a month old).

Sedative

A sedative is a substance that induces sedation by reducing irritability or excitement.

At higher doses it may result in slurred speech, staggering gait, poor judgment, and slow, uncertain reflexes. Doses of sedatives such as benzodiazepines when used as a hypnotic to induce sleep tend to be higher than those used to relieve anxiety whereas only low doses are needed to provide calming sedative effects.

Child development

Child development refers to the biological and psychological changes that occur in human beings between birth and the end of adolescence, as the individual progresses from dependency to increasing autonomy. Because these developmental changes may be strongly influenced by genetic factors and events during prenatal life, genetics and prenatal development are usually included as part of the study of child development. Related terms include developmental psychology, referring to development throughout the lifespan, and pediatrics, the branch of medicine relating to the care of children. Developmental change may occur as a result of genetically-controlled processes known as maturation, or as a result of environmental factors and learning, but most commonly involves an interaction between the two.

Lysergic acid diethylamide	Lysergic acid diethylamide is a semisynthetic psychedelic drug of the ergoline family, well known for its psychological effects which can include altered thinking processes, closed and open eye visuals, synaesthesia, an altered sense of time and spiritual experiences, as well as for its key role in 1960s counterculture. It is used mainly as an entheogen, recreational drug, and as an agent in psychedelic therapy. LSD is non-addictive, is not known to cause brain damage, and has extremely low toxicity relative to dose.
Bipolar disorder	Bipolar disorder, also referred to as bipolar affective disorder or manic depression, is a psychiatric diagnosis that describes a category of mood disorders defined by the presence of one or more episodes of abnormally elevated energy levels, cognition, and mood with or without one or more depressive episodes. The elevated moods are clinically referred to as mania or, if milder, hypomania. Individuals who experience manic episodes also commonly experience depressive episodes, or symptoms, or mixed episodes in which features of both mania and depression are present at the same time.
Lithium carbonate	Lithium carbonate is a chemical compound of lithium, carbon, and oxygen with the formula Li_2CO_3. This colorless salt is widely used in the processing of metal oxides and has received attention for its use in psychiatry. It is found in nature as the rare mineral zabuyelite.
Psychosis	Psychosis means abnormal condition of the mind, and is a generic psychiatric term for a mental state often described as involving a "loss of contact with reality". People suffering from psychosis are described as psychotic. Psychosis is given to the more severe forms of psychiatric disorder, during which hallucinations and delusions and impaired insight may occur.
Butyrophenone	Butyrophenone is a chemical compound (with a ketone functional group); some of its derivatives (called commonly butyrophenones) are used to treat various psychiatric disorders such as schizophrenia, as well as acting as antiemetics.
	Butyrophenones are a class of pharmaceutical drugs derived from butyrophenone.

Examples include:

- Haloperidol, the most widely used classical antipsychotic drug in this class
- Droperidol, often used for neuroleptanalgesic anesthesia and sedation in intensive-care treatment
- Benperidol, the most potent commonly-used antipsychotic (200 times more potent than chlorpromazine)
- Triperidol, a highly-potent antipsychotic (100 times more potent than chlorpromazine)
- Melperone, a weakly-potent antipsychotic, in Europe commonly used for treatment of insomnia, confusional states, psychomotor agitation, and delirium, in particular, in geriatric patients
- Lenperone
- Domperidone, a dopamine-antagonist antiemetic, derived further from butyrophenone.

The atypical antipsychotic risperidone, although not a butyrophenone, was developed with the structures of benperidol and lenperone as a basis.

Anticonvulsant

The anticonvulsants are a diverse group of pharmaceuticals used in the treatment of epileptic seizures. Anticonvulsants are also increasingly being used in the treatment of bipolar disorder, since many seem to act as mood stabilizers. The goal of an anticonvulsant is to suppress the rapid and excessive firing of neurons that start a seizure.

Schizophrenia

Schizophrenia is a mental disorder characterized by a disintegration of thought processes and of emotional responsiveness. It most commonly manifests as auditory hallucinations, paranoid or bizarre delusions, or disorganized speech and thinking, and it is accompanied by significant social or occupational dysfunction. The onset of symptoms typically occurs in young adulthood, with a global lifetime prevalence of about 0.3-0.7%.

Anxiety disorder

Anxiety disorders are blanket terms covering several different forms of abnormal and pathological fear and anxiety which only came under the aegis of psychiatry at the very end of the 19th century. Gelder, Mayou ' Geddes (2005) explains that anxiety disorders are classified in two groups: continuous symptoms and episodic symptoms. Current psychiatric diagnostic criteria recognize a wide variety of anxiety disorders.

Chapter 5. Treatment of abnormal states during pregnancy

Eating disorder	Eating disorders refer to a group of conditions characterized by abnormal eating habits that may involve either insufficient or excessive food intake to the detriment of an individual's physical and mental health. Binge eating disorder, bulimia nervosa, anorexia nervosa being the most common specific forms in the United States. Though primarily thought of as affecting females (an estimated 5-10 million being affected in the U.S)., eating disorders affect males as well (an estimated 1 million U.S. males being affected).
Substance abuse	Substance abuse refers to a maladaptive pattern of use of a substance that is not considered dependent. The term "drug abuse" does not exclude dependency, but is otherwise used in a similar manner in nonmedical contexts. The terms have a huge range of definitions related to taking a psychoactive drug or performance enhancing drug for a non-therapeutic or non-medical effect.
Behavior therapy	Behavior therapy is an approach to psychotherapy based on learning theory which aims to treat psychopathology through techniques designed to reinforce desired and eliminate undesired behaviors.
Pain	Pain is "an unpleasant sensory and emotional experience associated with actual or potential tissue damage, or described in terms of such damage." It is the feeling common to such experiences as stubbing a toe, burning a finger, putting iodine on a cut, and bumping the "funny bone". Pain motivates us to withdraw from potentially damaging situations, protect a damaged body part while it heals, and avoid those situations in the future. Most pain resolves promptly once the painful stimulus is removed and the body has healed, but sometimes pain persists despite removal of the stimulus and apparent healing of the body; and sometimes pain arises in the absence of any detectable stimulus, damage or disease.
Panic disorder	Panic disorder is an anxiety disorder characterized by recurring severe panic attacks. It may also include significant behavioral change lasting at least a month and of ongoing worry about the implications or concern about having other attacks. The latter are called anticipatory attacks (DSM-IVR).
Phobia	A phobia is an irrational, intense and persistent fear of certain situations, activities, things, animals, or people. The main symptom of this disorder is the excessive and unreasonable desire to avoid the feared stimulus. When the fear is beyond one's control, and if the fear is interfering with daily life, then a diagnosis under one of the anxiety disorders can be made.

Motivational interviewing	Motivational interviewing refers to a counseling approach in part developed by clinical psychologists Professor William R Miller, Ph.D. and Professor Stephen Rollnick, Ph.D. It is a client-centered, semi-directive method of engaging intrinsic motivation to change behavior by developing discrepancy and exploring and resolving ambivalence within the client. Motivational interviewing recognizes and accepts the fact that clients who need to make changes in their lives approach counseling at different levels of readiness to change their behavior. If the counseling is mandated, they may never have thought of changing the behavior in question.
Tokophobia	Tokophobia, is a form of specific phobia.
Anorexia nervosa	Anorexia nervosa is an eating disorder characterized by refusal to maintain a healthy body weight and an obsessive fear of gaining weight. It is often coupled with a distorted self image which may be maintained by various cognitive biases that alter how the affected individual evaluates and thinks about her or his body, food and eating. Persons with anorexia nervosa continue to feel hunger, but deny themselves all but very small quantities of food.
Clinical Global Impression	The Clinical Global Impression rating scales are commonly used measures of symptom severity, treatment response and the efficacy of treatments in treatment studies of patients with mental disorders (Guy, W., 1976). Many researchers, while recognizing the validity of the scale, consider it to be subjective as it requires the user of the scale to compare the subjects to typical patients in the clinician experience. The Clinical Global Impression - Severity scale (Clinical Global Impression-S)is a 7-point scale that requires the clinician to rate the severity of the patient's illness at the time of assessment, relative to the clinician's past experience with patients who have the same diagnosis.
Sexual abuse	Sexual abuse, also referred to as molestation, is the forcing of undesired sexual behavior by one person upon another. When that force is immediate, of short duration, or infrequent, it is called sexual assault. The offender is referred to as a sexual abuser or (often pejoratively) molester.

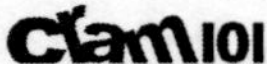

Intrusive thoughts	Intrusive thoughts are unwelcome involuntary thoughts, images, or unpleasant ideas that may become obsessions, are upsetting or distressing, and can be difficult to manage or eliminate. Most people experience these thoughts when they are associated with obsessive-compulsive disorder (OCD), depression, and sometimes attention-deficit hyperactive disorder (ADHD). They may become paralyzing, anxiety-provoking, or persistent.

Anxiety	Anxiety is a psychological and physiological state characterized by somatic, emotional, cognitive, and behavioral components. The root meaning of the word anxiety is 'to vex or trouble'; in either the absence or presence of psychological stress, anxiety can create feelings of fear, worry, uneasiness and dread. Anxiety is considered to be a normal reaction to stress.
Anxiety disorder	Anxiety disorders are blanket terms covering several different forms of abnormal and pathological fear and anxiety which only came under the aegis of psychiatry at the very end of the 19th century. Gelder, Mayou ' Geddes (2005) explains that anxiety disorders are classified in two groups: continuous symptoms and episodic symptoms. Current psychiatric diagnostic criteria recognize a wide variety of anxiety disorders.
Generalized anxiety disorder	Generalized anxiety disorder is an anxiety disorder that is characterized by excessive, uncontrollable and often irrational worry about everyday things that is disproportionate to the actual source of worry. This excessive worry often interferes with daily functioning, as individuals suffering Generalized anxiety disorder typically anticipate disaster, and are overly concerned about everyday matters such as health issues, money, death, family problems, friend problems, relationship problems or work difficulties. They often exhibit a variety of physical symptoms, including fatigue, fidgeting, headaches, nausea, numbness in hands and feet, muscle tension, muscle aches, difficulty swallowing, bouts of difficulty breathing, difficulty concentrating, trembling, twitching, irritability, agitation, sweating, restlessness, insomnia, hot flashes, and rashes and inability to fully control the anxiety.
Grief	Grief is a multi-faceted response to loss, particularly to the loss of someone or something to which a bond was formed. Although conventionally focused on the emotional response to loss, it also has physical, cognitive, behavioral, social, and philosophical dimensions. While the terms are often used interchangeably, bereavement often refers to the state of loss, and grief to the reaction to loss.
Depression	Depression is a state of low mood and aversion to activity that can affect a person's thoughts, behaviour, feelings and physical well-being. It may include feelings of sadness, anxiety, emptiness, hopelessness, worthlessness, guilt, irritability, or restlessness. Depressed people may lose interest in activities that once were pleasurable, experience difficulty concentrating, remembering details, or making decisions, and may contemplate or attempt suicide.
Attention deficit hyperactivity disorder	Attention deficit hyperactivity disorder is a neurobehavioral developmental disorder. It is primarily characterized by "the co-existence of attentional problems and hyperactivity, with each behavior occurring infrequently alone" and symptoms starting before seven years of age.

Attention deficit hyperactivity disorder is the most commonly studied and diagnosed psychiatric disorder in children, affecting about 3 to 5 percent of children globally and diagnosed in about 2 to 16 percent of school aged children.

Hyperactivity

Hyperactivity can be described as a physical state in which a person is abnormally and easily excitable or exuberant. Strong emotional reactions, impulsive behavior, and sometimes a short span of attention are also typical for a hyperactive person. Some individuals may show these characteristics naturally, as personality differs from person to person.

Infant

An infant is the very young offspring of humans. A newborn is an infant who is within hours, days, or up to a few weeks from birth. In medical contexts, newborn or neonate refers to an infant in the first 28 days of life (from birth up to 4 weeks after birth, less than a month old).

Abortion

Abortion is the termination of a pregnancy by the removal or expulsion of a fetus or embryo from the uterus, resulting in or caused by its death. An abortion can occur spontaneously due to complications during pregnancy or can be induced, in humans and other species. In the context of human pregnancies, an abortion induced to preserve the health of the gravida (pregnant female) is termed a therapeutic abortion, while an abortion induced for any other reason is termed an elective abortion.

Perspective

Perspective, in context of vision and visual perception, is the way in which objects appear to the eye based on their spatial attributes; or their dimensions and the position of the eye relative to the objects. There are two main meanings of the term: linear perspective and aerial perspective.

Linear perspective

As objects become more distant they appear smaller because their visual angle decreases.

Chapter 7. Parenting of the infant during the first year of life

Infant

An infant is the very young offspring of humans. A newborn is an infant who is within hours, days, or up to a few weeks from birth. In medical contexts, newborn or neonate refers to an infant in the first 28 days of life (from birth up to 4 weeks after birth, less than a month old).

Tokophobia

Tokophobia, is a form of specific phobia.

Regression

Regression, according to psychoanalyst Sigmund Freud, is a defense mechanism leading to the temporary or long-term reversion of the ego to an earlier stage of development rather than handling unacceptable impulses in a more adult way. The defense mechanism of regression, in psychoanalytic theory, occurs when thoughts are pushed back out of our consciousness and into our unconscious.

Freud, Regression, and Neurosis

Freud saw development, fixation, and regression as centrally formative elements in the creation of a neurosis.

Depression

Depression is a state of low mood and aversion to activity that can affect a person's thoughts, behaviour, feelings and physical well-being. It may include feelings of sadness, anxiety, emptiness, hopelessness, worthlessness, guilt, irritability, or restlessness. Depressed people may lose interest in activities that once were pleasurable, experience difficulty concentrating, remembering details, or making decisions, and may contemplate or attempt suicide.

Borderline personality disorder

Borderline personality disorder is a personality disorder described as a prolonged disturbance of personality function in a person (generally over the age of eighteen years, although it is also found in adolescents), characterized by depth and variability of moods. The disorder typically involves unusual levels of instability in mood; black and white thinking, or splitting; the disorder often manifests itself in idealization and devaluation episodes, as well as chaotic and unstable interpersonal relationships, self-image, identity, and behavior; as well as a disturbance in the individual's sense of self. In extreme cases, this disturbance in the sense of self can lead to periods of dissociation.

Infertility

Infertility primarily refers to the biological inability of a person to contribute to conception. Infertility may also refer to the state of a woman who is unable to carry a pregnancy to full term. There are many biological causes of infertility, some which may be bypassed with medical intervention.

Women who are fertile experience a natural period of fertility before and during ovulation, and they are naturally infertile during the rest of the menstrual cycle. Fertility awareness methods are used to discern when these changes occur by tracking changes in cervical mucus or basal body temperature.

Reuptake

Reuptake is the reabsorption of a neurotransmitter by a neurotransmitter transporter of a pre-synaptic neuron after it has performed its function of transmitting a neural impulse.

Reuptake is necessary for normal synaptic physiology because it allows for the recycling of neurotransmitters and regulates the level of neurotransmitter present in the synapse and controls how long a signal resulting from neurotransmitter release lasts. Because neurotransmitters are too large and hydrophilic to diffuse through the membrane, specific transport proteins are necessary for the reabsorption of neurotransmitters. Much research, both biochemical and structural, has been performed to obtain clues about the mechanism of reuptake.

Selective serotonin reuptake inhibitor

Selective serotonin reuptake inhibitors or serotonin-specific reuptake inhibitor are a class of compounds typically used as antidepressants in the treatment of depression, anxiety disorders, and some personality disorders. They are also typically effective and used in treating some cases of insomnia.

Selective serotonin reuptake inhibitors are believed to increase the extracellular level of the neurotransmitter serotonin by inhibiting its reuptake into the presynaptic cell, increasing the level of serotonin in the synaptic cleft available to bind to the postsynaptic receptor.

Serotonin

Serotonin is a monoamine neurotransmitter. Biochemically derived from tryptophan, serotonin is primarily found in the gastrointestinal (GI) tract, platelets, and in the central nervous system (CNS) of animals including humans. It is a well-known contributor to feelings of well-being; therefore it is also known as a "happiness hormone" despite not being a hormone.

Intervention

An intervention is an orchestrated attempt by one, or often many, people (usually family and friends) to get someone to seek professional help with an addiction or some kind of traumatic event or crisis, or other serious problem. The term intervention is most often used when the traumatic event involves addiction to drugs or other items. Intervention can also refer to the act of using a technique within a therapy session.

Chapter 7. Parenting of the infant during the first year of life

Psychosis

Psychosis means abnormal condition of the mind, and is a generic psychiatric term for a mental state often described as involving a "loss of contact with reality". People suffering from psychosis are described as psychotic. Psychosis is given to the more severe forms of psychiatric disorder, during which hallucinations and delusions and impaired insight may occur.

Paradigm

The word paradigm has been used in science to describe distinct concepts. It comes from Greek "παρ?δειγμα" (paradeigma), "pattern, example, sample" from the verb "παραδε?κνυμι" (paradeiknumi), "exhibit, represent, expose" and that from "παρ?" (para), "beside, by" + "δε?κνυμι" (deiknumi), "to show, to point out".

The original Greek term παραδε?γματι (paradeigma) was used in Greek texts such as Plato's Timaeus (28A) as the model or the pattern that the Demiurge (god) used to create the cosmos.

Stillbirth

A stillbirth occurs when a fetus has died in the uterus. The Australian definition specifies that fetal death is termed a stillbirth after 20 weeks gestation or the baby weighs more than 400 grams (14 oz). Once the baby has died the mother still has contractions and the baby is delivered. The term is often used in distinction to live birth or miscarriage. Most stillbirths occur in full term pregnancies.

Discipline

In its most general sense, discipline refers to systematic instruction given to a disciple. it is also known as sesencd witch means seasons or tempritrue. To discipline son to follow a particular code of conduct or "order".

Experience

Experience as a general concept comprises knowledge of or skill in or observation of some thing or some event gained through involvement in or exposure to that thing or event. The history of the word experience aligns it closely with the concept of experiment.

The concept of experience generally refers to know-how or procedural knowledge, rather than propositional knowledge: on-the-job training rather than book-learning.

Chapter 7. Parenting of the infant during the first year of life

Infant mental health	Infant mental health is the study of mental health as it applies to infants and their families. The field investigates optimal social and emotional development of infants and their families in the first three years of life. cognitive development, and the development of motor skills may also be considered part of the infant mental health picture.
Child Development	Child development refers to the biological and psychological changes that occur in human beings between birth and the end of adolescence, as the individual progresses from dependency to increasing autonomy. Because these developmental changes may be strongly influenced by genetic factors and events during prenatal life, genetics and prenatal development are usually included as part of the study of child development. Related terms include developmental psychology, referring to development throughout the lifespan, and pediatrics, the branch of medicine relating to the care of children. Developmental change may occur as a result of genetically-controlled processes known as maturation, or as a result of environmental factors and learning, but most commonly involves an interaction between the two.
Anxiety	Anxiety is a psychological and physiological state characterized by somatic, emotional, cognitive, and behavioral components. The root meaning of the word anxiety is 'to vex or trouble'; in either the absence or presence of psychological stress, anxiety can create feelings of fear, worry, uneasiness and dread. Anxiety is considered to be a normal reaction to stress.
Anxiety disorder	Anxiety disorders are blanket terms covering several different forms of abnormal and pathological fear and anxiety which only came under the aegis of psychiatry at the very end of the 19th century. Gelder, Mayou ' Geddes (2005) explains that anxiety disorders are classified in two groups: continuous symptoms and episodic symptoms. Current psychiatric diagnostic criteria recognize a wide variety of anxiety disorders.
Generalized anxiety disorder	Generalized anxiety disorder is an anxiety disorder that is characterized by excessive, uncontrollable and often irrational worry about everyday things that is disproportionate to the actual source of worry. This excessive worry often interferes with daily functioning, as individuals suffering Generalized anxiety disorder typically anticipate disaster, and are overly concerned about everyday matters such as health issues, money, death, family problems, friend problems, relationship problems or work difficulties. They often exhibit a variety of physical symptoms, including fatigue, fidgeting, headaches, nausea, numbness in hands and feet, muscle tension, muscle aches, difficulty swallowing, bouts of difficulty breathing, difficulty concentrating, trembling, twitching, irritability, agitation, sweating, restlessness, insomnia, hot flashes, and rashes and inability to fully control the anxiety.

Norepinephrine	Norepinephrine is a catecholamine with multiple roles including as a hormone and a neurotransmitter. As a stress hormone, norepinephrine affects parts of the brain, such as the amygdala, where attention and responses are controlled. Along with epinephrine, norepinephrine also underlies the fight-or-flight response, directly increasing heart rate, triggering the release of glucose from energy stores, and increasing blood flow to skeletal muscle. It increases the brain's oxygen supply. Norepinephrine can also suppress neuroinflammation when released diffusely in the brain from the locus ceruleus.
Psychotherapy	Psychotherapy is an intentional interpersonal relationship used by trained psychotherapists to aid a client or patient in problems of living. It is a talking therapy and aims to increase the individual's sense of their own well-being. Psychotherapists employ a range of techniques based on experiential relationship building, dialogue, communication and behavior change that are designed to improve the mental health of a client or patient, or to improve group relationships (such as in a family).
Relaxation technique	A relaxation technique is any method, process, procedure, or activity that helps a person to relax; to attain a state of increased calmness; or otherwise reduce levels of anxiety, stress or anger. Relaxation techniques are often employed as one element of a wider stress management program and can decrease muscle tension, lower the blood pressure and slow heart and breath rates, among other health benefits. Since the 1960s, research has indicated strong correlations between chronic stress and physical and emotional health.
Psychodynamics	Psychodynamics is the theory and systematic study of the psychological forces that underlie human behavior, especially the dynamic relations between conscious motivation and unconscious motivation. The psychologist Sigmund Freud (1856-1939) developed "psychodynamics" to describe the processes of the mind as flows of psychological energy (Libido) in an organically complex brain.

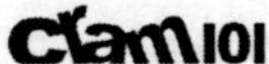

In medical praxis, psychodynamic psychotherapy is a less intensive, 3-5 weekly sessions, than the classical Freudian psychoanalysis treatment of only one weekly session.

Depression	Depression is a state of low mood and aversion to activity that can affect a person's thoughts, behaviour, feelings and physical well-being. It may include feelings of sadness, anxiety, emptiness, hopelessness, worthlessness, guilt, irritability, or restlessness. Depressed people may lose interest in activities that once were pleasurable, experience difficulty concentrating, remembering details, or making decisions, and may contemplate or attempt suicide.
Mental disorder	A mental disorder is a psychological or behavioral pattern generally associated with subjective distress or disability that occurs in an individual, and which is not a part of normal development or culture. The recognition and understanding of mental health conditions has changed over time and across cultures, and there are still variations in the definition, assessment, and classification of mental disorders, although standard guideline criteria are widely accepted. A few mental disorders are diagnosed based on the harm to others, regardless of the subject's perception of distress.
Infant	An infant is the very young offspring of humans. A newborn is an infant who is within hours, days, or up to a few weeks from birth. In medical contexts, newborn or neonate refers to an infant in the first 28 days of life (from birth up to 4 weeks after birth, less than a month old).
Infant mental health	Infant mental health is the study of mental health as it applies to infants and their families. The field investigates optimal social and emotional development of infants and their families in the first three years of life. cognitive development, and the development of motor skills may also be considered part of the infant mental health picture.
Infertility	Infertility primarily refers to the biological inability of a person to contribute to conception. Infertility may also refer to the state of a woman who is unable to carry a pregnancy to full term. There are many biological causes of infertility, some which may be bypassed with medical intervention. Women who are fertile experience a natural period of fertility before and during ovulation, and they are naturally infertile during the rest of the menstrual cycle. Fertility awareness methods are used to discern when these changes occur by tracking changes in cervical mucus or basal body temperature.
Mania	Mania, the presence of which is a criterion for certain psychiatric diagnoses, is a state of abnormally elevated or irritable mood, arousal, and/or energy levels. In a sense, it is the opposite of depression.

In addition to mood disorders, individuals may exhibit manic behavior as a result of drug intoxication (notably stimulants such as cocaine or methamphetamine), medication side effects (notably steroids), or malignancy.

Motivation

Motivation is the driving force which causes us to achieve goals. Motivation is said to be intrinsic or extrinsic. The term is generally used for humans but, theoretically, it can also be used to describe the causes for animal behavior as well.

Psychosis

Psychosis means abnormal condition of the mind, and is a generic psychiatric term for a mental state often described as involving a "loss of contact with reality". People suffering from psychosis are described as psychotic. Psychosis is given to the more severe forms of psychiatric disorder, during which hallucinations and delusions and impaired insight may occur.

Reuptake

Reuptake is the reabsorption of a neurotransmitter by a neurotransmitter transporter of a pre-synaptic neuron after it has performed its function of transmitting a neural impulse.

Reuptake is necessary for normal synaptic physiology because it allows for the recycling of neurotransmitters and regulates the level of neurotransmitter present in the synapse and controls how long a signal resulting from neurotransmitter release lasts. Because neurotransmitters are too large and hydrophilic to diffuse through the membrane, specific transport proteins are necessary for the reabsorption of neurotransmitters. Much research, both biochemical and structural, has been performed to obtain clues about the mechanism of reuptake.

Selective serotonin reuptake inhibitor

Selective serotonin reuptake inhibitors or serotonin-specific reuptake inhibitor are a class of compounds typically used as antidepressants in the treatment of depression, anxiety disorders, and some personality disorders. They are also typically effective and used in treating some cases of insomnia.

Selective serotonin reuptake inhibitors are believed to increase the extracellular level of the neurotransmitter serotonin by inhibiting its reuptake into the presynaptic cell, increasing the level of serotonin in the synaptic cleft available to bind to the postsynaptic receptor.

Serotonin	Serotonin is a monoamine neurotransmitter. Biochemically derived from tryptophan, serotonin is primarily found in the gastrointestinal (GI) tract, platelets, and in the central nervous system (CNS) of animals including humans. It is a well-known contributor to feelings of well-being; therefore it is also known as a "happiness hormone" despite not being a hormone.
Nicotine	Nicotine is an alkaloid found in the nightshade family of plants (Solanaceae) that constitutes approximately 0.6-3.0% of the dry weight of tobacco, with biosynthesis taking place in the roots and accumulation occurring in the leaves. It functions as an antiherbivore chemical with particular specificity to insects; therefore nicotine was widely used as an insecticide in the past, and currently nicotine analogs such as imidacloprid continue to be widely used. Nicotine is also found in several other members of the Solanaceae family, with small amounts being present in species such as the eggplant and tomato.
Smoking	Smoking is a practice in which a substance, most commonly tobacco or cannabis, is burned and the smoke is tasted or inhaled. This is primarily practised as a route of administration for recreational drug use, as combustion releases the active substances in drugs such as nicotine and makes them available for absorption through the lungs. It can also be done as a part of rituals, to induce trances and spiritual enlightenment.
Self-confidence	The socio-psychological concept of self-confidence relates to self-assuredness in one's personal judgment, ability, power, etc., sometimes manifested excessively. Promise yourself, no matter how difficult the problem life throws at you, that you will try as hard as you can to help yourself. You acknowledge that sometimes your efforts to help yourself may not result in success, as often being properly rewarded is not in your control.
Fetal alcohol syndrome	Fetal/Foetal alcohol syndrome is a pattern of mental and physical defects that can develop in a fetus when a woman drinks alcohol during pregnancy. The timing and frequency of alcohol consumption during pregnancy are major factors in the risk of a child developing fetal alcohol syndrome. While the ingestion of alcohol does not always result in Fetal alcohol syndrome, there are no medically established guidelines for safe levels of alcohol consumption during pregnancy.
Intrusive thoughts	Intrusive thoughts are unwelcome involuntary thoughts, images, or unpleasant ideas that may become obsessions, are upsetting or distressing, and can be difficult to manage or eliminate. Most people experience these thoughts when they are associated with obsessive-compulsive disorder (OCD), depression, and sometimes attention-deficit hyperactive disorder (ADHD). They may become paralyzing, anxiety-provoking, or persistent.

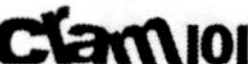

Chapter 8. Parental risk factors for parenthood

Child abuse	Child abuse is the physical, sexual, emotional mistreatment, or neglect of children. In the United States, the Centers for Disease Control and Prevention (CDC) define child maltreatment as any act or series of acts of commission or omission by a parent or other caregiver that results in harm, potential for harm, or threat of harm to a child. Most child abuse occurs in a child's home, with a smaller amount occurring in the organizations, schools or communities the child interacts with.
Child development	Child development refers to the biological and psychological changes that occur in human beings between birth and the end of adolescence, as the individual progresses from dependency to increasing autonomy. Because these developmental changes may be strongly influenced by genetic factors and events during prenatal life, genetics and prenatal development are usually included as part of the study of child development. Related terms include developmental psychology, referring to development throughout the lifespan, and pediatrics, the branch of medicine relating to the care of children. Developmental change may occur as a result of genetically-controlled processes known as maturation, or as a result of environmental factors and learning, but most commonly involves an interaction between the two.
Antipsychotic	An antipsychotic is a tranquilizing psychiatric medication primarily used to manage psychosis (including delusions or hallucinations, as well as disordered thought), particularly in schizophrenia and bipolar disorder. A first generation of antipsychotics, known as typical antipsychotics, was discovered in the 1950s. Most of the drugs in the second generation, known as atypical antipsychotics, have been developed more recently, although the first atypical antipsychotic, clozapine, was discovered in the 1950s and introduced clinically in the 1970s.
Antisocial personality disorder	Antisocial personality disorder is defined by the American Psychiatric Association's Diagnostic and Statistical Manual as "...a pervasive pattern of disregard for, and violation of, the rights of others that begins in childhood or early adolescence and continues into adulthood." Antisocial personality disorder is sometimes referred to as psychopathy or sociopathy. However, these two are not the same. Rather, psychopathy and sociopathy are generally considered subsets of ASPD. Some researchers believe that ASPD and psychopathy may be separate conditions altogether.
Tokophobia	Tokophobia, is a form of specific phobia.

Intervention

An intervention is an orchestrated attempt by one, or often many, people (usually family and friends) to get someone to seek professional help with an addiction or some kind of traumatic event or crisis, or other serious problem. The term intervention is most often used when the traumatic event involves addiction to drugs or other items. Intervention can also refer to the act of using a technique within a therapy session.

Substance abuse

Substance abuse refers to a maladaptive pattern of use of a substance that is not considered dependent. The term "drug abuse" does not exclude dependency, but is otherwise used in a similar manner in nonmedical contexts. The terms have a huge range of definitions related to taking a psychoactive drug or performance enhancing drug for a non-therapeutic or non-medical effect.

Health effect

Health effects are changes in health resulting from exposure to a source. Health effects are an important consideration in many areas, such as hygiene, pollution studies, workplace safety, nutrition and health sciences in general. Some of the major environmental sources of health effects are air pollution, water pollution, soil contamination, noise pollution and over-illumination.

Withdrawal

Withdrawal can refer to any sort of separation, but is most commonly used to describe the group of symptoms that occurs upon the abrupt discontinuation/separation or a decrease in dosage of the intake of medications, recreational drugs, and/or alcohol. In order to experience the symptoms of withdrawal, one must have first developed a physical dependence (often referred to as chemical dependency). This happens after consuming one or more of these substances for a certain period of time, which is both dose dependent and varies based upon the drug consumed.

Addiction

Historically, addiction has been defined as physical and psychological dependence on psychoactive substances (for example alcohol, tobacco, heroin and other drugs) which cross the blood-brain barrier once ingested, temporarily altering the chemical milieu of the brain.

Addiction can also be viewed as a continued involvement with a substance or activity despite the negative consequences associated with it. Pleasure and enjoyment would have originally been sought, however over a period of time involvement with the substance or activity is needed to feel normal.

Chapter 8. Parental risk factors for parenthood

Attention deficit hyperactivity disorder	Attention deficit hyperactivity disorder is a neurobehavioral developmental disorder. It is primarily characterized by "the co-existence of attentional problems and hyperactivity, with each behavior occurring infrequently alone" and symptoms starting before seven years of age. Attention deficit hyperactivity disorder is the most commonly studied and diagnosed psychiatric disorder in children, affecting about 3 to 5 percent of children globally and diagnosed in about 2 to 16 percent of school aged children.
Developmental disorder	Developmental disorders are disorders that occur at some stage in a child's development, often retarding the development. These may include psychological or physical disorders. They can be grouped into specific developmental disorder and pervasive developmental disorders.
Hyperactivity	Hyperactivity can be described as a physical state in which a person is abnormally and easily excitable or exuberant. Strong emotional reactions, impulsive behavior, and sometimes a short span of attention are also typical for a hyperactive person. Some individuals may show these characteristics naturally, as personality differs from person to person.
Alcohol Use Disorders Identification Test	The Alcohol Use Disorders Identification Test is a simple ten-question test developed by the World Health Organization to determine if a person's alcohol consumption may be harmful. The test was designed to be used internationally, and was validated in a study using patients from six countries. Questions 1-3 deal with alcohol consumption, 4-6 relate to alcohol dependence and 7-10 consider alcohol related problems.
CAGE questionnaire	The CAGE questionnaire, the name of which is an acronym of its four questions, is a widely used method of screening for alcoholism.

Two "yes" responses indicate that the respondent should be investigated further. The questionnaire asks the following questions:

1. Have you ever felt you needed to Cut down on your drinking?
2. Have people Annoyed you by criticizing your drinking?
3. Have you ever felt Guilty about drinking?
4. Have you ever felt you needed a drink first thing in the morning (Eye-opener) to steady your nerves or to get rid of a hangover?

The CAGE questionnaire, among other methods, has been extensively validated for use in identifying alcoholism.

Identification

Identification is a psychological process whereby the subject assimilates an aspect, property, or attribute of the other and is transformed, wholly or partially, after the model the other provides. It is by means of a series of identifications that the personality is constituted and specified. The roots of the concept can be found in Freud's writings.

Antidepressant

An antidepressant is a psychiatric medication used to alleviate mood disorders, such as major depression and dysthymia and anxiety disorders such as social anxiety disorder. According to Gelder, Mayou '*Geddes (2005) people with a depressive illness will experience a therapeutic effect to their mood, however this will not be experienced in healthy individuals. Drugs including the monoamine oxidase inhibitors (MAOIs), tricyclic antidepressants (TCAs), tetracyclic antidepressants (TeCAs), selective serotonin reuptake inhibitors (SSRIs), and serotonin-norepinephrine reuptake inhibitors (SNRIs) are most commonly associated with the term.

Tricyclic antidepressant

Tricyclic antidepressants (TCAs) are heterocyclic chemical compounds used primarily as antidepressants. The TCAs were first discovered in the early 1950s and were subsequently introduced later in the decade; since then the ability of the trycyclics to relieve depressive symptoms has been firmly established. They are named after their chemical structure, which contains three rings of atoms. The tetracyclic antidepressants (TeCAs), which contain four rings of atoms, are a closely related group of antidepressant compounds.

Norepinephrine

Norepinephrine is a catecholamine with multiple roles including as a hormone and a neurotransmitter.

As a stress hormone, norepinephrine affects parts of the brain, such as the amygdala, where attention and responses are controlled. Along with epinephrine, norepinephrine also underlies the fight-or-flight response, directly increasing heart rate, triggering the release of glucose from energy stores, and increasing blood flow to skeletal muscle. It increases the brain's oxygen supply. Norepinephrine can also suppress neuroinflammation when released diffusely in the brain from the locus ceruleus.

Depression	Depression is a state of low mood and aversion to activity that can affect a person's thoughts, behaviour, feelings and physical well-being. It may include feelings of sadness, anxiety, emptiness, hopelessness, worthlessness, guilt, irritability, or restlessness. Depressed people may lose interest in activities that once were pleasurable, experience difficulty concentrating, remembering details, or making decisions, and may contemplate or attempt suicide.
Representation	Representation is a term used in cognitive psychology, neuroscience, and cognitive science to refer to a hypothetical internal cognitive symbol that represents external reality. David Marr defines representation as "a formal system for making explicit certain entities or types of information, together with a specification of how the system does this." Representationalism (also known as indirect realism) is the view that representations are the main way we access external reality.
Intervention	An intervention is an orchestrated attempt by one, or often many, people (usually family and friends) to get someone to seek professional help with an addiction or some kind of traumatic event or crisis, or other serious problem. The term intervention is most often used when the traumatic event involves addiction to drugs or other items. Intervention can also refer to the act of using a technique within a therapy session.
Mental disorder	A mental disorder is a psychological or behavioral pattern generally associated with subjective distress or disability that occurs in an individual, and which is not a part of normal development or culture. The recognition and understanding of mental health conditions has changed over time and across cultures, and there are still variations in the definition, assessment, and classification of mental disorders, although standard guideline criteria are widely accepted. A few mental disorders are diagnosed based on the harm to others, regardless of the subject's perception of distress.
Nicotine	Nicotine is an alkaloid found in the nightshade family of plants (Solanaceae) that constitutes approximately 0.6-3.0% of the dry weight of tobacco, with biosynthesis taking place in the roots and accumulation occurring in the leaves. It functions as an antiherbivore chemical with particular specificity to insects; therefore nicotine was widely used as an insecticide in the past, and currently nicotine analogs such as imidacloprid continue to be widely used. Nicotine is also found in several other members of the Solanaceae family, with small amounts being present in species such as the eggplant and tomato.
Smoking	Smoking is a practice in which a substance, most commonly tobacco or cannabis, is burned and the smoke is tasted or inhaled. This is primarily practised as a route of administration for recreational drug use, as combustion releases the active substances in drugs such as nicotine and makes them available for absorption through the lungs. It can also be done as a part of rituals, to induce trances and spiritual enlightenment.

Prenatal stress	Prenatal stress is exposure of an expectant mother to distress, which can be caused by stressful life events or by environmental hardships. The resulting changes to the mother's hormonal and immune system may harm the fetus's (and after birth, the infant's) immune function and brain development.
Sibling	Siblings are people who share at least one parent. A male sibling is called a brother; and a female sibling is called a sister. In most societies throughout the world, siblings usually grow up together and spend a good deal of their childhood socializing with one another. This genetic and physical closeness may be marked by the development of strong emotional bond such as love or enmity. The emotional bond between siblings is often complicated and is influenced by factors such as parental treatment, birth order, personality, and personal experiences outside the family.
Developmental disorder	Developmental disorders are disorders that occur at some stage in a child's development, often retarding the development. These may include psychological or physical disorders. They can be grouped into specific developmental disorder and pervasive developmental disorders.
Extrapyramidal symptoms	The extrapyramidal system can be affected in a number of ways, which are revealed in a range of extrapyramidal symptoms also known as extrapyramidal side-effects (EPSE), such as akinesia (inability to initiate movement) and akathisia (inability to remain motionless). Extrapyramidal symptoms are various movement disorders such as acute dystonic reactions, pseudoparkinsonism, or akathisia suffered as a result of taking dopamine antagonists, usually antipsychotic (neuroleptic) drugs, which are often used to control psychosis. The Simpson-Angus Scale (SAS) and the Barnes Akathisia Rating Scale (BARS) are used to measure extrapyramidal symptoms.

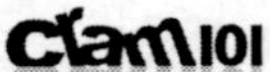

Denial

Denial is a defense mechanism postulated by Sigmund Freud, in which a person is faced with a fact that is too uncomfortable to accept and rejects it instead, insisting that it is not true despite what may be overwhelming evidence. The subject may use:

- simple denial - deny the reality of the unpleasant fact altogether
- minimisation - admit the fact but deny its seriousness (a combination of denial and rationalisation), or
- projection - admit both the fact and seriousness but deny responsibility.

The concept of denial is particularly important to the study of addiction. The theory of denial was first researched seriously by Anna Freud.

Incest

Incest is sexual intercourse between close relatives that is illegal in the jurisdiction where it takes place and/or is socially taboo. The type of sexual activity and the nature of the relationship between people that constitutes a breach of law or social taboo vary with culture and jurisdiction. Some societies consider incest to include only those who live in the same household, or who belong to the same clan or lineage; other societies consider it to include "blood relatives"; other societies further include those related by adoption or marriage.

Infant

An infant is the very young offspring of humans. A newborn is an infant who is within hours, days, or up to a few weeks from birth. In medical contexts, newborn or neonate refers to an infant in the first 28 days of life (from birth up to 4 weeks after birth, less than a month old).

Acquaintance rape

Acquaintance rape is an assault or attempted assault usually committed by a new acquaintance involving sexual intercourse without mutual consent.

The term "date rape" is widely used but can be misleading because the person who commits the crime might not be dating the victim. Rather, it could be an acquaintance or stranger.

Chapter 9. Environmental risk factors for parenthood

Abortion

Abortion is the termination of a pregnancy by the removal or expulsion of a fetus or embryo from the uterus, resulting in or caused by its death. An abortion can occur spontaneously due to complications during pregnancy or can be induced, in humans and other species. In the context of human pregnancies, an abortion induced to preserve the health of the gravida (pregnant female) is termed a therapeutic abortion, while an abortion induced for any other reason is termed an elective abortion.

Infertility

Infertility primarily refers to the biological inability of a person to contribute to conception. Infertility may also refer to the state of a woman who is unable to carry a pregnancy to full term. There are many biological causes of infertility, some which may be bypassed with medical intervention. Women who are fertile experience a natural period of fertility before and during ovulation, and they are naturally infertile during the rest of the menstrual cycle. Fertility awareness methods are used to discern when these changes occur by tracking changes in cervical mucus or basal body temperature.

Relaxation technique

A relaxation technique is any method, process, procedure, or activity that helps a person to relax; to attain a state of increased calmness; or otherwise reduce levels of anxiety, stress or anger. Relaxation techniques are often employed as one element of a wider stress management program and can decrease muscle tension, lower the blood pressure and slow heart and breath rates, among other health benefits.

Since the 1960s, research has indicated strong correlations between chronic stress and physical and emotional health.

Reuptake

Reuptake is the reabsorption of a neurotransmitter by a neurotransmitter transporter of a pre-synaptic neuron after it has performed its function of transmitting a neural impulse.

Reuptake is necessary for normal synaptic physiology because it allows for the recycling of neurotransmitters and regulates the level of neurotransmitter present in the synapse and controls how long a signal resulting from neurotransmitter release lasts. Because neurotransmitters are too large and hydrophilic to diffuse through the membrane, specific transport proteins are necessary for the reabsorption of neurotransmitters. Much research, both biochemical and structural, has been performed to obtain clues about the mechanism of reuptake.

Selective serotonin reuptake inhibitor	Selective serotonin reuptake inhibitors or serotonin-specific reuptake inhibitor are a class of compounds typically used as antidepressants in the treatment of depression, anxiety disorders, and some personality disorders. They are also typically effective and used in treating some cases of insomnia. Selective serotonin reuptake inhibitors are believed to increase the extracellular level of the neurotransmitter serotonin by inhibiting its reuptake into the presynaptic cell, increasing the level of serotonin in the synaptic cleft available to bind to the postsynaptic receptor.
Serotonin	Serotonin is a monoamine neurotransmitter. Biochemically derived from tryptophan, serotonin is primarily found in the gastrointestinal (GI) tract, platelets, and in the central nervous system (CNS) of animals including humans. It is a well-known contributor to feelings of well-being; therefore it is also known as a "happiness hormone" despite not being a hormone.
Attention deficit hyperactivity disorder	Attention deficit hyperactivity disorder is a neurobehavioral developmental disorder. It is primarily characterized by "the co-existence of attentional problems and hyperactivity, with each behavior occurring infrequently alone" and symptoms starting before seven years of age. Attention deficit hyperactivity disorder is the most commonly studied and diagnosed psychiatric disorder in children, affecting about 3 to 5 percent of children globally and diagnosed in about 2 to 16 percent of school aged children.
Hyperactivity	Hyperactivity can be described as a physical state in which a person is abnormally and easily excitable or exuberant. Strong emotional reactions, impulsive behavior, and sometimes a short span of attention are also typical for a hyperactive person. Some individuals may show these characteristics naturally, as personality differs from person to person.
Anorexia nervosa	Anorexia nervosa is an eating disorder characterized by refusal to maintain a healthy body weight and an obsessive fear of gaining weight. It is often coupled with a distorted self image which may be maintained by various cognitive biases that alter how the affected individual evaluates and thinks about her or his body, food and eating. Persons with anorexia nervosa continue to feel hunger, but deny themselves all but very small quantities of food.

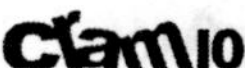

Clinical Global Impression	The Clinical Global Impression rating scales are commonly used measures of symptom severity, treatment response and the efficacy of treatments in treatment studies of patients with mental disorders (Guy, W., 1976). Many researchers, while recognizing the validity of the scale, consider it to be subjective as it requires the user of the scale to compare the subjects to typical patients in the clinician experience. The Clinical Global Impression - Severity scale (Clinical Global Impression-S)is a 7-point scale that requires the clinician to rate the severity of the patient's illness at the time of assessment, relative to the clinician's past experience with patients who have the same diagnosis.
Child development	Child development refers to the biological and psychological changes that occur in human beings between birth and the end of adolescence, as the individual progresses from dependency to increasing autonomy. Because these developmental changes may be strongly influenced by genetic factors and events during prenatal life, genetics and prenatal development are usually included as part of the study of child development. Related terms include developmental psychology, referring to development throughout the lifespan, and pediatrics, the branch of medicine relating to the care of children. Developmental change may occur as a result of genetically-controlled processes known as maturation, or as a result of environmental factors and learning, but most commonly involves an interaction between the two.
Burnout	Burnout is a psychological term for the experience of long-term exhaustion and diminished interest. Research indicates general practitioners have the highest proportion of burnout cases (according to a recent Dutch study in Psychological Reports, no less than 40% of these experienced high levels of burnout). Burnout is not a recognized disorder in the DSM although it is recognized in the ICD-10 as "Problems related to life-management difficulty".
Child abuse	Child abuse is the physical, sexual, emotional mistreatment, or neglect of children. In the United States, the Centers for Disease Control and Prevention (CDC) define child maltreatment as any act or series of acts of commission or omission by a parent or other caregiver that results in harm, potential for harm, or threat of harm to a child. Most child abuse occurs in a child's home, with a smaller amount occurring in the organizations, schools or communities the child interacts with.
Coping strategies	The German Freudian psychoanalyst Karen Horney defined four so-called coping strategies to define interpersonal relations, one describing psychologically healthy individuals, the others describing neurotic states.

	These are the strategies in which psychologically healthy people develop relationships. It involves compromise. In order to move with, there must be communication, agreement, disagreement, compromise, and decisions.
Mental health	Mental health describes either a level of cognitive or emotional well-being or an absence of a mental disorder. From perspectives of the discipline of positive psychology or holism mental health may include an individual's ability to enjoy life and procure a balance between life activities and efforts to achieve psychological resilience. Mental health is an expression of our emotions and signifies a successful adaptation to a range of demands.
Sexual abuse	Sexual abuse, also referred to as molestation, is the forcing of undesired sexual behavior by one person upon another. When that force is immediate, of short duration, or infrequent, it is called sexual assault. The offender is referred to as a sexual abuser or (often pejoratively) molester.
Norepinephrine	Norepinephrine is a catecholamine with multiple roles including as a hormone and a neurotransmitter. As a stress hormone, norepinephrine affects parts of the brain, such as the amygdala, where attention and responses are controlled. Along with epinephrine, norepinephrine also underlies the fight-or-flight response, directly increasing heart rate, triggering the release of glucose from energy stores, and increasing blood flow to skeletal muscle. It increases the brain's oxygen supply. Norepinephrine can also suppress neuroinflammation when released diffusely in the brain from the locus ceruleus.
Tokophobia	Tokophobia, is a form of specific phobia.
Recovery model	The Recovery Model as it applies to mental health is an approach to mental disorder or substance dependence (and/or from being labeled in those terms) that emphasizes and supports each individual's potential for recovery. Recovery is seen within the model as a personal journey, that may involve developing hope, a secure base and sense of self, supportive relationships, empowerment, social inclusion, coping skills, and meaning. Originating from the 12-Step Program of Alcoholics Anonymous and the Civil Rights Movement, the use of the concept in mental health emerged as deinstitutionalization resulted in more individuals living in the community.

Chapter 9. Environmental risk factors for parenthood

Capacity

The capacity of both natural and legal persons determines whether they may make binding amendments to their rights, duties and obligations, such as getting married or merging, entering into contracts, making gifts, or writing a valid will. Capacity is an aspect of status and both are defined by a person's personal law:

- for natural persons, the law of domicile or lex domicilii in common law jurisdictions, and either the law of nationality or lex patriae, or of habitual residence in civil law states;
- for legal persons, the law of the place of incorporation, the lex incorporationis for companies while other forms of business entity derive their capacity either from the law of the place in which they were formed or the laws of the states in which they establish a presence for trading purposes depending on the nature of the entity and the transactions entered into.

When the law limits or bars a person from engaging in specified activities, any agreements or contracts to do so are either voidable or void for incapacity. Sometimes such legal incapacity is referred to as incompetence.

Motivational interviewing

Motivational interviewing refers to a counseling approach in part developed by clinical psychologists Professor William R Miller, Ph.D. and Professor Stephen Rollnick, Ph.D. It is a client-centered, semi-directive method of engaging intrinsic motivation to change behavior by developing discrepancy and exploring and resolving ambivalence within the client.

Motivational interviewing recognizes and accepts the fact that clients who need to make changes in their lives approach counseling at different levels of readiness to change their behavior. If the counseling is mandated, they may never have thought of changing the behavior in question.

Perspective

Perspective, in context of vision and visual perception, is the way in which objects appear to the eye based on their spatial attributes; or their dimensions and the position of the eye relative to the objects. There are two main meanings of the term: linear perspective and aerial perspective.

Linear perspective

	As objects become more distant they appear smaller because their visual angle decreases.
Domestic violence	Domestic violence can be broadly defined as a pattern of abusive behaviors by one or both partners in an intimate relationship such as marriage, dating, family, friends or cohabitation. Domestic violence has many forms including physical aggression (hitting, kicking, biting, shoving, restraining, slapping, throwing objects), or threats thereof; sexual abuse; emotional abuse; controlling or domineering; intimidation; stalking; passive/covert abuse (e.g., neglect); and economic deprivation. Alcohol consumption and mental illness can be co-morbid with abuse, and present additional challenges when present alongside patterns of abuse.
Fetal alcohol syndrome	Fetal/Foetal alcohol syndrome is a pattern of mental and physical defects that can develop in a fetus when a woman drinks alcohol during pregnancy. The timing and frequency of alcohol consumption during pregnancy are major factors in the risk of a child developing fetal alcohol syndrome. While the ingestion of alcohol does not always result in Fetal alcohol syndrome, there are no medically established guidelines for safe levels of alcohol consumption during pregnancy.
Intrusive thoughts	Intrusive thoughts are unwelcome involuntary thoughts, images, or unpleasant ideas that may become obsessions, are upsetting or distressing, and can be difficult to manage or eliminate. Most people experience these thoughts when they are associated with obsessive-compulsive disorder (OCD), depression, and sometimes attention-deficit hyperactive disorder (ADHD). They may become paralyzing, anxiety-provoking, or persistent.

Chapter 10. Assessment of parenthood

Nicotine

Nicotine is an alkaloid found in the nightshade family of plants (Solanaceae) that constitutes approximately 0.6-3.0% of the dry weight of tobacco, with biosynthesis taking place in the roots and accumulation occurring in the leaves. It functions as an antiherbivore chemical with particular specificity to insects; therefore nicotine was widely used as an insecticide in the past, and currently nicotine analogs such as imidacloprid continue to be widely used. Nicotine is also found in several other members of the Solanaceae family, with small amounts being present in species such as the eggplant and tomato.

Representation

Representation is a term used in cognitive psychology, neuroscience, and cognitive science to refer to a hypothetical internal cognitive symbol that represents external reality. David Marr defines representation as "a formal system for making explicit certain entities or types of information, together with a specification of how the system does this." Representationalism (also known as indirect realism) is the view that representations are the main way we access external reality.

Smoking

Smoking is a practice in which a substance, most commonly tobacco or cannabis, is burned and the smoke is tasted or inhaled. This is primarily practised as a route of administration for recreational drug use, as combustion releases the active substances in drugs such as nicotine and makes them available for absorption through the lungs. It can also be done as a part of rituals, to induce trances and spiritual enlightenment.

Clinical Global Impression

The Clinical Global Impression rating scales are commonly used measures of symptom severity, treatment response and the efficacy of treatments in treatment studies of patients with mental disorders (Guy, W., 1976). Many researchers, while recognizing the validity of the scale, consider it to be subjective as it requires the user of the scale to compare the subjects to typical patients in the clinician experience.

The Clinical Global Impression - Severity scale (Clinical Global Impression-S)is a 7-point scale that requires the clinician to rate the severity of the patient's illness at the time of assessment, relative to the clinician's past experience with patients who have the same diagnosis.

Depression

Depression is a state of low mood and aversion to activity that can affect a person's thoughts, behaviour, feelings and physical well-being. It may include feelings of sadness, anxiety, emptiness, hopelessness, worthlessness, guilt, irritability, or restlessness. Depressed people may lose interest in activities that once were pleasurable, experience difficulty concentrating, remembering details, or making decisions, and may contemplate or attempt suicide.

Monoamine oxidase inhibitor	Monoamine oxidase inhibitors (MAOIs) are a class of antidepressant drugs prescribed for the treatment of depression. They are particularly effective in treating atypical depression. Because of potentially lethal dietary and drug interactions, monoamine oxidase inhibitors have historically been reserved as a last line of treatment, used only when other classes of antidepressant drugs (for example selective serotonin reuptake inhibitors and tricyclic antidepressants) have failed.
Infant	An infant is the very young offspring of humans. A newborn is an infant who is within hours, days, or up to a few weeks from birth. In medical contexts, newborn or neonate refers to an infant in the first 28 days of life (from birth up to 4 weeks after birth, less than a month old).
Lactation	Lactation describes the secretion of milk from the mammary glands, the process of providing that milk to the young, and the period of time that a mother lactates to feed her young. The process occurs in all female mammals, and in humans it is commonly referred to as breastfeeding or nursing. In most species milk comes out of the mother's nipples; however, the platypus (a non-placental mammal) releases milk through ducts in its abdomen.
Contingency management	Contingency management is a type of treatment used in the mental health or substance abuse fields. Patients are rewarded (or, less often, punished) for their behavior; generally, adherence to or failure to adhere to program rules and regulations or their treatment plan. For children with conduct disorder, token systems are highly successful but do not help the children achieve normal functioning unless combined with a cost response program reinforcing negative punishment.
Individual differences psychology	The science of psychology studies people at three levels of focus captured by the well known quote: "Every man is in certain respects (a) like all other men, (b) like some other men, (c) like no other man". Individual differences psychology focuses on this second level of study. It is also sometimes called Differential Psychology because researchers in this area study the ways in which individual people differ in their behavior. This is distinguished from other aspects of psychology in that although psychology is ostensibly a study of individuals, modern psychologists often study groups or biological underpinnings of cognition.

Cognition	Cognition is the scientific term for "the process of thought". Usage of the term varies in different disciplines; for example in psychology and cognitive science, it usually refers to an information processing view of an individual's psychological functions. Other interpretations of the meaning of cognition link it to the development of concepts; individual minds, groups, and organizations.
Intervention	An intervention is an orchestrated attempt by one, or often many, people (usually family and friends) to get someone to seek professional help with an addiction or some kind of traumatic event or crisis, or other serious problem. The term intervention is most often used when the traumatic event involves addiction to drugs or other items. Intervention can also refer to the act of using a technique within a therapy session.
Child Development	Child development refers to the biological and psychological changes that occur in human beings between birth and the end of adolescence, as the individual progresses from dependency to increasing autonomy. Because these developmental changes may be strongly influenced by genetic factors and events during prenatal life, genetics and prenatal development are usually included as part of the study of child development. Related terms include developmental psychology, referring to development throughout the lifespan, and pediatrics, the branch of medicine relating to the care of children. Developmental change may occur as a result of genetically-controlled processes known as maturation, or as a result of environmental factors and learning, but most commonly involves an interaction between the two.
Psychosis	Psychosis means abnormal condition of the mind, and is a generic psychiatric term for a mental state often described as involving a "loss of contact with reality". People suffering from psychosis are described as psychotic. Psychosis is given to the more severe forms of psychiatric disorder, during which hallucinations and delusions and impaired insight may occur.
Social support	Social support is the physical and emotional comfort given to us by our family, friends, co-workers and others. It is knowing that we are part of a community of people who love and care for us, and value and think well of us. Social support is a way of categorizing the rewards of communication in a particular circumstance. An important aspect of support is that a message or communicative experience does not constitute support unless the receiver views it as such.
Mental health	Mental health describes either a level of cognitive or emotional well-being or an absence of a mental disorder. From perspectives of the discipline of positive psychology or holism mental health may include an individual's ability to enjoy life and procure a balance between life activities and efforts to achieve psychological resilience. Mental health is an expression of our emotions and signifies a successful adaptation to a range of demands.

Mental health professional

A mental health professional is a person who offers services for the purpose of improving an individual's mental health or to treat mental illness. This broad category includes psychiatrists, clinical psychologists, licensed professional counselors, clinical social workers, psychiatric nurses, mental health counselors as well as many other professionals. These professionals often deal with the same illnesses, disorders, conditions, and issues; however their scope of practice often differs.

Capacity

The capacity of both natural and legal persons determines whether they may make binding amendments to their rights, duties and obligations, such as getting married or merging, entering into contracts, making gifts, or writing a valid will. Capacity is an aspect of status and both are defined by a person's personal law:

- for natural persons, the law of domicile or lex domicilii in common law jurisdictions, and either the law of nationality or lex patriae, or of habitual residence in civil law states;
- for legal persons, the law of the place of incorporation, the lex incorporationis for companies while other forms of business entity derive their capacity either from the law of the place in which they were formed or the laws of the states in which they establish a presence for trading purposes depending on the nature of the entity and the transactions entered into.

When the law limits or bars a person from engaging in specified activities, any agreements or contracts to do so are either voidable or void for incapacity. Sometimes such legal incapacity is referred to as incompetence.

Therapeutic Jurisprudence

Therapeutic jurisprudence is a term first used by Professor David Wexler, University of Arizona Rogers College of Law and University of Puerto Rico School of Law, in a paper delivered to the National Institute of Mental Health in 1987. Along with Professor Bruce Winick, University of Miami School of Law, who originated the concept with Wexler, the professors suggested the need for a new perspective, Therapeutic jurisprudence, to study the extent to which substantive rules, legal procedures, and the role of legal actors (lawyers and judges primarily) produce therapeutic or antitherapeutic consequences for individuals involved in the legal process.

Black's Law Dictionary, 9th edition, 2009, defines 'therapeutic jurisprudence' as: "The study of the effects of law and the legal system on the behavior, emotions, and mental health of people: esp, a multidisciplinary examination of how law and mental health interact. This discipline originated in the late 1980s as an academic approach to mental health law."

History

In the early 90's, legal scholars began to use it when discussing mental health law, including Wexler and Winick's 1991 book, Essays in Therapeutic Jurisprudence.

Antidepressant

An antidepressant is a psychiatric medication used to alleviate mood disorders, such as major depression and dysthymia and anxiety disorders such as social anxiety disorder. According to Gelder, Mayou '*Geddes (2005) people with a depressive illness will experience a therapeutic effect to their mood, however this will not be experienced in healthy individuals. Drugs including the monoamine oxidase inhibitors (MAOIs), tricyclic antidepressants (TCAs), tetracyclic antidepressants (TeCAs), selective serotonin reuptake inhibitors (SSRIs), and serotonin-norepinephrine reuptake inhibitors (SNRIs) are most commonly associated with the term.

Infertility

Infertility primarily refers to the biological inability of a person to contribute to conception. Infertility may also refer to the state of a woman who is unable to carry a pregnancy to full term. There are many biological causes of infertility, some which may be bypassed with medical intervention. Women who are fertile experience a natural period of fertility before and during ovulation, and they are naturally infertile during the rest of the menstrual cycle. Fertility awareness methods are used to discern when these changes occur by tracking changes in cervical mucus or basal body temperature.

Reuptake

Reuptake is the reabsorption of a neurotransmitter by a neurotransmitter transporter of a pre-synaptic neuron after it has performed its function of transmitting a neural impulse.

Reuptake is necessary for normal synaptic physiology because it allows for the recycling of neurotransmitters and regulates the level of neurotransmitter present in the synapse and controls how long a signal resulting from neurotransmitter release lasts. Because neurotransmitters are too large and hydrophilic to diffuse through the membrane, specific transport proteins are necessary for the reabsorption of neurotransmitters. Much research, both biochemical and structural, has been performed to obtain clues about the mechanism of reuptake.

Selective serotonin reuptake inhibitor

Selective serotonin reuptake inhibitors or serotonin-specific reuptake inhibitor are a class of compounds typically used as antidepressants in the treatment of depression, anxiety disorders, and some personality disorders. They are also typically effective and used in treating some cases of insomnia.

Selective serotonin reuptake inhibitors are believed to increase the extracellular level of the neurotransmitter serotonin by inhibiting its reuptake into the presynaptic cell, increasing the level of serotonin in the synaptic cleft available to bind to the postsynaptic receptor.

Serotonin

Serotonin is a monoamine neurotransmitter. Biochemically derived from tryptophan, serotonin is primarily found in the gastrointestinal (GI) tract, platelets, and in the central nervous system (CNS) of animals including humans. It is a well-known contributor to feelings of well-being; therefore it is also known as a "happiness hormone" despite not being a hormone.

Intervention

An intervention is an orchestrated attempt by one, or often many, people (usually family and friends) to get someone to seek professional help with an addiction or some kind of traumatic event or crisis, or other serious problem. The term intervention is most often used when the traumatic event involves addiction to drugs or other items. Intervention can also refer to the act of using a technique within a therapy session.

Beck Depression Inventory

The Beck Depression Inventory created by Dr. Aaron T. Beck, is a 21-question multiple-choice self-report inventory, one of the most widely used instruments for measuring the severity of depression. Its development marked a shift among health care professionals, who had until then viewed depression from a psychodynamic perspective, instead of it being rooted in the patient's own thoughts.

In its current version the questionnaire is designed for individuals aged 13 and over, and is composed of items relating to symptoms of depression such as hopelessness and irritability, cognitions such as guilt or feelings of being punished, as well as physical symptoms such as fatigue, weight loss, and lack of interest in sex.

Depression

Depression is a state of low mood and aversion to activity that can affect a person's thoughts, behaviour, feelings and physical well-being. It may include feelings of sadness, anxiety, emptiness, hopelessness, worthlessness, guilt, irritability, or restlessness. Depressed people may lose interest in activities that once were pleasurable, experience difficulty concentrating, remembering details, or making decisions, and may contemplate or attempt suicide.

Anxiolytic

An anxiolytic is a drug used for the treatment of anxiety, and its related psychological and physical symptoms. Anxiolytics have been shown to be useful in the treatment of anxiety disorders.

Beta-receptor blockers such as propranolol and oxprenolol, although not anxiolytics, can be used to combat the somatic symptoms of anxiety.

Benzodiazepine

A benzodiazepine is a psychoactive drug whose core chemical structure is the fusion of a benzene ring and a diazepine ring. The first benzodiazepine, chlordiazepoxide (Librium), was discovered accidentally by Leo Sternbach in 1955, and made available in 1960 by Hoffmann-La Roche, which has also marketed diazepam (Valium) since 1963.

Infant

An infant is the very young offspring of humans. A newborn is an infant who is within hours, days, or up to a few weeks from birth. In medical contexts, newborn or neonate refers to an infant in the first 28 days of life (from birth up to 4 weeks after birth, less than a month old).

Child development

Child development refers to the biological and psychological changes that occur in human beings between birth and the end of adolescence, as the individual progresses from dependency to increasing autonomy. Because these developmental changes may be strongly influenced by genetic factors and events during prenatal life, genetics and prenatal development are usually included as part of the study of child development. Related terms include developmental psychology, referring to development throughout the lifespan, and pediatrics, the branch of medicine relating to the care of children. Developmental change may occur as a result of genetically-controlled processes known as maturation, or as a result of environmental factors and learning, but most commonly involves an interaction between the two.

Butyrophenone

Butyrophenone is a chemical compound (with a ketone functional group); some of its derivatives (called commonly butyrophenones) are used to treat various psychiatric disorders such as schizophrenia, as well as acting as antiemetics.

Butyrophenones are a class of pharmaceutical drugs derived from butyrophenone.

Examples include:

- Haloperidol, the most widely used classical antipsychotic drug in this class
- Droperidol, often used for neuroleptanalgesic anesthesia and sedation in intensive-care treatment
- Benperidol, the most potent commonly-used antipsychotic (200 times more potent than chlorpromazine)
- Triperidol, a highly-potent antipsychotic (100 times more potent than chlorpromazine)
- Melperone, a weakly-potent antipsychotic, in Europe commonly used for treatment of insomnia, confusional states, psychomotor agitation, and delirium, in particular, in geriatric patients
- Lenperone
- Domperidone, a dopamine-antagonist antiemetic, derived further from butyrophenone.

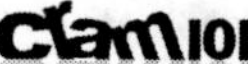

The atypical antipsychotic risperidone, although not a butyrophenone, was developed with the structures of benperidol and lenperone as a basis.

Anticonvulsant

The anticonvulsants are a diverse group of pharmaceuticals used in the treatment of epileptic seizures. Anticonvulsants are also increasingly being used in the treatment of bipolar disorder, since many seem to act as mood stabilizers. The goal of an anticonvulsant is to suppress the rapid and excessive firing of neurons that start a seizure.

Bipolar disorder

Bipolar disorder, also referred to as bipolar affective disorder or manic depression, is a psychiatric diagnosis that describes a category of mood disorders defined by the presence of one or more episodes of abnormally elevated energy levels, cognition, and mood with or without one or more depressive episodes. The elevated moods are clinically referred to as mania or, if milder, hypomania. Individuals who experience manic episodes also commonly experience depressive episodes, or symptoms, or mixed episodes in which features of both mania and depression are present at the same time.

Lithium carbonate

Lithium carbonate is a chemical compound of lithium, carbon, and oxygen with the formula Li_2CO_3. This colorless salt is widely used in the processing of metal oxides and has received attention for its use in psychiatry. It is found in nature as the rare mineral zabuyelite.

Ambivalence

Ambivalence is a state of having simultaneous, conflicting feelings toward a person or thing. Stated another way, ambivalence is the experience of having thoughts and emotions of both positive and negative valence toward someone or something. A common example of ambivalence is the feeling of both love and hate for a person.

Amphetamine

Amphetamine is a psychostimulant drug of the phenethylamine class that is known to produce increased wakefulness and focus in association with decreased fatigue and appetite. Brand names of medications that contain, or metabolize into, amphetamine include Adderall, Dexedrine, Dextrostat, Desoxyn, ProCentra, and Vyvanse, as well as Benzedrine in the past.

Antidepressant

An antidepressant is a psychiatric medication used to alleviate mood disorders, such as major depression and dysthymia and anxiety disorders such as social anxiety disorder. According to Gelder, Mayou '*Geddes (2005) people with a depressive illness will experience a therapeutic effect to their mood, however this will not be experienced in healthy individuals. Drugs including the monoamine oxidase inhibitors (MAOIs), tricyclic antidepressants (TCAs), tetracyclic antidepressants (TeCAs), selective serotonin reuptake inhibitors (SSRIs), and serotonin-norepinephrine reuptake inhibitors (SNRIs) are most commonly associated with the term.

Chapter 11. Treatment of dysfunctional parenting

Behavior therapy	Behavior therapy is an approach to psychotherapy based on learning theory which aims to treat psychopathology through techniques designed to reinforce desired and eliminate undesired behaviors.
Stimulant	Stimulants (also called psychostimulants) are psychoactive drugs which induce temporary improvements in either mental or physical function or both. Examples of these kinds of effects may include enhanced alertness, wakefulness, and locomotion, among others. Due to their effects typically having an "up" quality to them, stimulants are also occasionally referred to as "uppers".
Nicotine	Nicotine is an alkaloid found in the nightshade family of plants (Solanaceae) that constitutes approximately 0.6-3.0% of the dry weight of tobacco, with biosynthesis taking place in the roots and accumulation occurring in the leaves. It functions as an antiherbivore chemical with particular specificity to insects; therefore nicotine was widely used as an insecticide in the past, and currently nicotine analogs such as imidacloprid continue to be widely used. Nicotine is also found in several other members of the Solanaceae family, with small amounts being present in species such as the eggplant and tomato.
Norepinephrine	Norepinephrine is a catecholamine with multiple roles including as a hormone and a neurotransmitter. As a stress hormone, norepinephrine affects parts of the brain, such as the amygdala, where attention and responses are controlled. Along with epinephrine, norepinephrine also underlies the fight-or-flight response, directly increasing heart rate, triggering the release of glucose from energy stores, and increasing blood flow to skeletal muscle. It increases the brain's oxygen supply. Norepinephrine can also suppress neuroinflammation when released diffusely in the brain from the locus ceruleus.
Reuptake	Reuptake is the reabsorption of a neurotransmitter by a neurotransmitter transporter of a pre-synaptic neuron after it has performed its function of transmitting a neural impulse. Reuptake is necessary for normal synaptic physiology because it allows for the recycling of neurotransmitters and regulates the level of neurotransmitter present in the synapse and controls how long a signal resulting from neurotransmitter release lasts. Because neurotransmitters are too large and hydrophilic to diffuse through the membrane, specific transport proteins are necessary for the reabsorption of neurotransmitters. Much research, both biochemical and structural, has been performed to obtain clues about the mechanism of reuptake.

Smoking	Smoking is a practice in which a substance, most commonly tobacco or cannabis, is burned and the smoke is tasted or inhaled. This is primarily practised as a route of administration for recreational drug use, as combustion releases the active substances in drugs such as nicotine and makes them available for absorption through the lungs. It can also be done as a part of rituals, to induce trances and spiritual enlightenment.
Mental health	Mental health describes either a level of cognitive or emotional well-being or an absence of a mental disorder. From perspectives of the discipline of positive psychology or holism mental health may include an individual's ability to enjoy life and procure a balance between life activities and efforts to achieve psychological resilience. Mental health is an expression of our emotions and signifies a successful adaptation to a range of demands.
Anxiety	Anxiety is a psychological and physiological state characterized by somatic, emotional, cognitive, and behavioral components. The root meaning of the word anxiety is 'to vex or trouble'; in either the absence or presence of psychological stress, anxiety can create feelings of fear, worry, uneasiness and dread. Anxiety is considered to be a normal reaction to stress.
Anxiety disorder	Anxiety disorders are blanket terms covering several different forms of abnormal and pathological fear and anxiety which only came under the aegis of psychiatry at the very end of the 19th century. Gelder, Mayou ' Geddes (2005) explains that anxiety disorders are classified in two groups: continuous symptoms and episodic symptoms. Current psychiatric diagnostic criteria recognize a wide variety of anxiety disorders.
Generalized anxiety disorder	Generalized anxiety disorder is an anxiety disorder that is characterized by excessive, uncontrollable and often irrational worry about everyday things that is disproportionate to the actual source of worry. This excessive worry often interferes with daily functioning, as individuals suffering Generalized anxiety disorder typically anticipate disaster, and are overly concerned about everyday matters such as health issues, money, death, family problems, friend problems, relationship problems or work difficulties. They often exhibit a variety of physical symptoms, including fatigue, fidgeting, headaches, nausea, numbness in hands and feet, muscle tension, muscle aches, difficulty swallowing, bouts of difficulty breathing, difficulty concentrating, trembling, twitching, irritability, agitation, sweating, restlessness, insomnia, hot flashes, and rashes and inability to fully control the anxiety.

Group psychotherapy	Group psychotherapy is a form of psychotherapy in which one or more therapists treat a small group of clients together as a group. The term can legitimately refer to any form of psychotherapy when delivered in a group format, including Cognitive behavioural therapy or Interpersonal therapy, but it is usually applied to psychodynamic group therapy where the group context and group process is explicitly utilised as a mechanism of change by developing, exploring and examining interpersonal relationships within the group. The broader concept of group therapy can be taken to include any helping process that takes place in a group, including support groups, skills training groups (such as anger management, mindfulness, relaxation training or social skills training), and psycho-education groups.
Motivational interviewing	Motivational interviewing refers to a counseling approach in part developed by clinical psychologists Professor William R Miller, Ph.D. and Professor Stephen Rollnick, Ph.D. It is a client-centered, semi-directive method of engaging intrinsic motivation to change behavior by developing discrepancy and exploring and resolving ambivalence within the client. Motivational interviewing recognizes and accepts the fact that clients who need to make changes in their lives approach counseling at different levels of readiness to change their behavior. If the counseling is mandated, they may never have thought of changing the behavior in question.

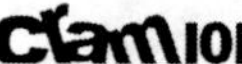

Intervention	An intervention is an orchestrated attempt by one, or often many, people (usually family and friends) to get someone to seek professional help with an addiction or some kind of traumatic event or crisis, or other serious problem. The term intervention is most often used when the traumatic event involves addiction to drugs or other items. Intervention can also refer to the act of using a technique within a therapy session.
Anxiety	Anxiety is a psychological and physiological state characterized by somatic, emotional, cognitive, and behavioral components. The root meaning of the word anxiety is 'to vex or trouble'; in either the absence or presence of psychological stress, anxiety can create feelings of fear, worry, uneasiness and dread. Anxiety is considered to be a normal reaction to stress.
Anxiety disorder	Anxiety disorders are blanket terms covering several different forms of abnormal and pathological fear and anxiety which only came under the aegis of psychiatry at the very end of the 19th century. Gelder, Mayou ' Geddes (2005) explains that anxiety disorders are classified in two groups: continuous symptoms and episodic symptoms. Current psychiatric diagnostic criteria recognize a wide variety of anxiety disorders.
Borderline personality disorder	Borderline personality disorder is a personality disorder described as a prolonged disturbance of personality function in a person (generally over the age of eighteen years, although it is also found in adolescents), characterized by depth and variability of moods. The disorder typically involves unusual levels of instability in mood; black and white thinking, or splitting; the disorder often manifests itself in idealization and devaluation episodes, as well as chaotic and unstable interpersonal relationships, self-image, identity, and behavior; as well as a disturbance in the individual's sense of self. In extreme cases, this disturbance in the sense of self can lead to periods of dissociation.
Generalized anxiety disorder	Generalized anxiety disorder is an anxiety disorder that is characterized by excessive, uncontrollable and often irrational worry about everyday things that is disproportionate to the actual source of worry. This excessive worry often interferes with daily functioning, as individuals suffering Generalized anxiety disorder typically anticipate disaster, and are overly concerned about everyday matters such as health issues, money, death, family problems, friend problems, relationship problems or work difficulties. They often exhibit a variety of physical symptoms, including fatigue, fidgeting, headaches, nausea, numbness in hands and feet, muscle tension, muscle aches, difficulty swallowing, bouts of difficulty breathing, difficulty concentrating, trembling, twitching, irritability, agitation, sweating, restlessness, insomnia, hot flashes, and rashes and inability to fully control the anxiety.
Infertility	Infertility primarily refers to the biological inability of a person to contribute to conception. Infertility may also refer to the state of a woman who is unable to carry a pregnancy to full term. There are many biological causes of infertility, some which may be bypassed with medical intervention.

Women who are fertile experience a natural period of fertility before and during ovulation, and they are naturally infertile during the rest of the menstrual cycle. Fertility awareness methods are used to discern when these changes occur by tracking changes in cervical mucus or basal body temperature.

Paradigm

The word paradigm has been used in science to describe distinct concepts. It comes from Greek "παρ?δειγμα" (paradeigma), "pattern, example, sample" from the verb "παραδε?κνυμι" (paradeiknumi), "exhibit, represent, expose" and that from "παρ?" (para), "beside, by" + "δε?κνυμι" (deiknumi), "to show, to point out".

The original Greek term παραδε?γματι (paradeigma) was used in Greek texts such as Plato's Timaeus (28A) as the model or the pattern that the Demiurge (god) used to create the cosmos.

Reuptake

Reuptake is the reabsorption of a neurotransmitter by a neurotransmitter transporter of a pre-synaptic neuron after it has performed its function of transmitting a neural impulse.

Reuptake is necessary for normal synaptic physiology because it allows for the recycling of neurotransmitters and regulates the level of neurotransmitter present in the synapse and controls how long a signal resulting from neurotransmitter release lasts. Because neurotransmitters are too large and hydrophilic to diffuse through the membrane, specific transport proteins are necessary for the reabsorption of neurotransmitters. Much research, both biochemical and structural, has been performed to obtain clues about the mechanism of reuptake.

Selective serotonin reuptake inhibitor

Selective serotonin reuptake inhibitors or serotonin-specific reuptake inhibitor are a class of compounds typically used as antidepressants in the treatment of depression, anxiety disorders, and some personality disorders. They are also typically effective and used in treating some cases of insomnia.

Selective serotonin reuptake inhibitors are believed to increase the extracellular level of the neurotransmitter serotonin by inhibiting its reuptake into the presynaptic cell, increasing the level of serotonin in the synaptic cleft available to bind to the postsynaptic receptor.

Chapter 12. Pathological parenting: from the infant`s perspective

Serotonin	Serotonin is a monoamine neurotransmitter. Biochemically derived from tryptophan, serotonin is primarily found in the gastrointestinal (GI) tract, platelets, and in the central nervous system (CNS) of animals including humans. It is a well-known contributor to feelings of well-being; therefore it is also known as a "happiness hormone" despite not being a hormone.
Stillbirth	A stillbirth occurs when a fetus has died in the uterus. The Australian definition specifies that fetal death is termed a stillbirth after 20 weeks gestation or the baby weighs more than 400 grams (14 oz). Once the baby has died the mother still has contractions and the baby is delivered. The term is often used in distinction to live birth or miscarriage. Most stillbirths occur in full term pregnancies.
Mental health	Mental health describes either a level of cognitive or emotional well-being or an absence of a mental disorder. From perspectives of the discipline of positive psychology or holism mental health may include an individual's ability to enjoy life and procure a balance between life activities and efforts to achieve psychological resilience. Mental health is an expression of our emotions and signifies a successful adaptation to a range of demands.
Infant	An infant is the very young offspring of humans. A newborn is an infant who is within hours, days, or up to a few weeks from birth. In medical contexts, newborn or neonate refers to an infant in the first 28 days of life (from birth up to 4 weeks after birth, less than a month old).
Alcohol Use Disorders Identification Test	The Alcohol Use Disorders Identification Test is a simple ten-question test developed by the World Health Organization to determine if a person's alcohol consumption may be harmful. The test was designed to be used internationally, and was validated in a study using patients from six countries. Questions 1-3 deal with alcohol consumption, 4-6 relate to alcohol dependence and 7-10 consider alcohol related problems.
Identification	Identification is a psychological process whereby the subject assimilates an aspect, property, or attribute of the other and is transformed, wholly or partially, after the model the other provides. It is by means of a series of identifications that the personality is constituted and specified. The roots of the concept can be found in Freud's writings.
Affect	Affect refers to the experience of feeling or emotion. Affect is a key part of the process of an organism's interaction with stimuli. The word also refers sometimes to affect display, which is "a facial, vocal, or gestural behavior that serves as an indicator of affect".

Chapter 12. Pathological parenting: from the infant`s perspective

Intrusive thoughts	Intrusive thoughts are unwelcome involuntary thoughts, images, or unpleasant ideas that may become obsessions, are upsetting or distressing, and can be difficult to manage or eliminate. Most people experience these thoughts when they are associated with obsessive-compulsive disorder (OCD), depression, and sometimes attention-deficit hyperactive disorder (ADHD). They may become paralyzing, anxiety-provoking, or persistent.
Representation	Representation is a term used in cognitive psychology, neuroscience, and cognitive science to refer to a hypothetical internal cognitive symbol that represents external reality. David Marr defines representation as "a formal system for making explicit certain entities or types of information, together with a specification of how the system does this." Representationalism (also known as indirect realism) is the view that representations are the main way we access external reality.
Tokophobia	Tokophobia, is a form of specific phobia.
Depression	Depression is a state of low mood and aversion to activity that can affect a person's thoughts, behaviour, feelings and physical well-being. It may include feelings of sadness, anxiety, emptiness, hopelessness, worthlessness, guilt, irritability, or restlessness. Depressed people may lose interest in activities that once were pleasurable, experience difficulty concentrating, remembering details, or making decisions, and may contemplate or attempt suicide.
Countertransference	Countertransference is defined as redirection of a psychotherapist's feelings toward a client--or, more generally, as a therapist's emotional entanglement with a client. Early Formulations
	The phenomenon was first defined by Sigmund Freud in 1910 in "The Future Prospects of Psycho-Analytic Therapy" as "a result of the patient's influence on [the physician's] unconscious feelings," but the topic was left to others to develop, as he rarely referred to it himself.. When he did, it was almost invariably in terms of a 'warning against any countertransference lying in wait' for the analyst: 'every psychoanalyst...must recognize this countertransference in himself and master it'.

Chapter 13. Mental health infant health in resource-constrained settings:

Depression

Depression is a state of low mood and aversion to activity that can affect a person's thoughts, behaviour, feelings and physical well-being. It may include feelings of sadness, anxiety, emptiness, hopelessness, worthlessness, guilt, irritability, or restlessness. Depressed people may lose interest in activities that once were pleasurable, experience difficulty concentrating, remembering details, or making decisions, and may contemplate or attempt suicide.

Infant

An infant is the very young offspring of humans. A newborn is an infant who is within hours, days, or up to a few weeks from birth. In medical contexts, newborn or neonate refers to an infant in the first 28 days of life (from birth up to 4 weeks after birth, less than a month old).

Mental health

Mental health describes either a level of cognitive or emotional well-being or an absence of a mental disorder. From perspectives of the discipline of positive psychology or holism mental health may include an individual's ability to enjoy life and procure a balance between life activities and efforts to achieve psychological resilience. Mental health is an expression of our emotions and signifies a successful adaptation to a range of demands.

Health promotion

Health promotion has been defined by the World Health Organization's 2005 Bangkok Charter for Health Promotion in a Globalized World as "the process of enabling people to increase control over their health and its determinants, and thereby improve their health". The primary means of health promotion occur through developing healthy public policy that addresses the prerequisities of health such as income, housing, food security, employment, and quality working conditions. There is a tendency among public health officials and governments--and this is especially the case in liberal nations such as Canada and the USA--to reduce health promotion to health education and social marketing focused on changing behavioral risk factors.

Human rights

Human rights are "rights and freedoms to which all humans are entitled." Proponents of the concept usually assert that everyone is endowed with certain entitlements merely by reason of being human. Human rights are thus conceived in a universalist and egalitarian fashion. Such entitlements can exist as shared norms of actual human moralities, as justified moral norms or natural rights supported by strong reasons, or as legal rights either at a national level or within international law.

Child Development	Child development refers to the biological and psychological changes that occur in human beings between birth and the end of adolescence, as the individual progresses from dependency to increasing autonomy. Because these developmental changes may be strongly influenced by genetic factors and events during prenatal life, genetics and prenatal development are usually included as part of the study of child development. Related terms include developmental psychology, referring to development throughout the lifespan, and pediatrics, the branch of medicine relating to the care of children. Developmental change may occur as a result of genetically-controlled processes known as maturation, or as a result of environmental factors and learning, but most commonly involves an interaction between the two.
Anxiety	Anxiety is a psychological and physiological state characterized by somatic, emotional, cognitive, and behavioral components. The root meaning of the word anxiety is 'to vex or trouble'; in either the absence or presence of psychological stress, anxiety can create feelings of fear, worry, uneasiness and dread. Anxiety is considered to be a normal reaction to stress.
Anxiety disorder	Anxiety disorders are blanket terms covering several different forms of abnormal and pathological fear and anxiety which only came under the aegis of psychiatry at the very end of the 19th century. Gelder, Mayou ' Geddes (2005) explains that anxiety disorders are classified in two groups: continuous symptoms and episodic symptoms. Current psychiatric diagnostic criteria recognize a wide variety of anxiety disorders.
Generalized anxiety disorder	Generalized anxiety disorder is an anxiety disorder that is characterized by excessive, uncontrollable and often irrational worry about everyday things that is disproportionate to the actual source of worry. This excessive worry often interferes with daily functioning, as individuals suffering Generalized anxiety disorder typically anticipate disaster, and are overly concerned about everyday matters such as health issues, money, death, family problems, friend problems, relationship problems or work difficulties. They often exhibit a variety of physical symptoms, including fatigue, fidgeting, headaches, nausea, numbness in hands and feet, muscle tension, muscle aches, difficulty swallowing, bouts of difficulty breathing, difficulty concentrating, trembling, twitching, irritability, agitation, sweating, restlessness, insomnia, hot flashes, and rashes and inability to fully control the anxiety.

Group psychotherapy	Group psychotherapy is a form of psychotherapy in which one or more therapists treat a small group of clients together as a group. The term can legitimately refer to any form of psychotherapy when delivered in a group format, including Cognitive behavioural therapy or Interpersonal therapy, but it is usually applied to psychodynamic group therapy where the group context and group process is explicitly utilised as a mechanism of change by developing, exploring and examining interpersonal relationships within the group. The broader concept of group therapy can be taken to include any helping process that takes place in a group, including support groups, skills training groups (such as anger management, mindfulness, relaxation training or social skills training), and psycho-education groups.

Lightning Source UK Ltd.
Milton Keynes UK
UKOW03f0821060515

250965UK00004B/57/P